The Coming FINANCIAL CRISIS

A look behind the WIZARD'S CURTAIN

D0861509

JOHN TRUMAN WOLFE

Lisa Hagan Books

Disclaimer
All statements, comments, and opinions expressed are solely those of the author and are subject to change without notice. They are written for the purpose of educating the reader. This is not a solicitation for the purchase or sale of any securities or options on securities, and it does not constitute a recommendation to you or to any specific person of any particular action. This book is intended to educate, not to provide investment or other types of advice. All factual information has been obtained from sources the writer believed to be reliable, and all effort has been made to cite all sources. The accuracy and completeness of the factual information is not guaranteed. Please notify the publisher if a source is quoted and not cited. Not all investments are right for everyone. You should conduct your own research and/or consult your investment or other advisor before making any investment.

Excerpts by Matt Taibbi From *Rolling Stone*, July 9-23, 2009
© Rolling Stone LLC 2009

All Rights Reserved. Reprinted by Permission.
ISBN: 978-0-9969686-4-5 (paperback)
Library of Congress Cataloging-in-Publication Data
CIP Date available upon request.
Publisher: Lisa Hagan Books

For information about special discounts for bulk purchases, please reach us through, www.lisahaganbooks.com

Cover design by Smythtype Design

Photo credits: istock.com/James Brey; Branislav; Tuned_In

Praise for Crisis by Design

"Wolfe cuts through the smoke and noise and connects some big and ugly dots, documenting his thesis that a cynical international banking cabal has actually engineered one of the greatest global financial squeeze plays yet, in order to extend its already-pervasive political, economic and mental control over the U.S. and other economies and populations. Does such a cynical cabal truly exist? Can the people behind the scenes pulling the strings be truly so selfish and evil? Wolfe mounts a plausible case for an affirmative answer. At the least, readers can get a startling insight into the 'game behind the game,' and how the world of 'the major players' and the shadowy 'kingmakers' might really work. Wolfe pulls no punches and names plenty of names. An eye-opening and educational read."

—Michael Baybak, Financial PR Executive

"Until the true facts of any scene are uncovered and the hidden agendas exposed, the Financial Crisis will continue like the dark clouds over Mordor. The price to pay for such an exposé is astute observation that spans decades. This story can't be understood in a snap-shot. The undermining of America, the Freedom she stands for and the US dollar is a scheme that has played out for decades....

"The final question is: Will America have the backbone to rid itself of such repugnant criminals and fix the system before she....? I trust with all my heart the answer is yes. Read the book! Then act!"

—Ned McCrink, Entrepreneur Orange County, CA

"Wolfe has done a spectacular job of clearly and logically explaining the real reasons behind our current problems with inflation, the housing crisis and our economy. His understanding of the subject comes out of 30 years of experience as a financial advisor and one-time banker, and it is this breadth of understanding, coupled with a curious and meticulous mind, that provides the reader with a clear look 'behind the curtain'."

—Alex Eckelberry, CEO—Sunbelt Software

"John Truman Wolfe is a first class writer and political commentator who possesses a huge intellect and never ending passion to expose the ills that plague our society. He is an ombudsman for the common man."

—Terry Jastrow, Seven Time Emmy-Award-Winning Producer/Director

"Very few individuals understand the enormity of the subversive and destructive impact on our civilization that originates from the money controllers and manipulators.

John Truman Wolfe not only understands but has thoroughly documented this situation and identified those responsible. More importantly, he has communicated the data in a way that anyone can understand.

For anyone desiring financial freedom, the material authored by Wolfe is so vital that it can be truly stated that financial freedom is impossible without a fundamental command of this data.

That is what Wolfe delivers."

—Larry Byrnes, CEO, Competence Software

"Thank you for the enlightenment. Your laser of truth will penetrate all the lies and expose the truth which we suffer in short supply. You have helped others expand their value as citizens of this great nation."

—Dr. Conrad Maulfair

"You are providing an essential understanding here. We, as 'citizens,' need to understand the increased danger of the age-old game now being played out on a worldwide level—the exploitation by the 'few' of the labor and property of the many. Thank you for a clear view!"

—Glen Wahlquist

"Your observations are so refreshing (to the point of chilling) in correctly targeting the key elements and developments! What a bracing antidote to the murky misdirections of the news media."

—Tom Hall, TH Travel

"I was missing the real scene of what the Bank for International Settlements does, and what REALLY happened. You name names. You give a simple chronology of the events leading to our financial woes. You fill in the details that I've never seen. You pulled the cover off an amazing tangle of lies and deceits. I applaud you loudly for your well-thought-out and well-written works.

—Dave Kluge, Author, *The People's Guide to the United States Constitution*

To the Friends of Liberty

Table of Contents

PREFACE

Throughout America's tumultuous history, there has been a tradition in its literature and letters of compiling essays, articles, pamphlets, etc., into books so that readers could get the sometimes urgent messages in one place and quickly.

Speed was critical because the information these various forms of writing held was vital to the issues at hand—at least that was the conclusion I reached as I sat reading essay after essay, letter after letter, in my apartment in Brooklyn as I worked on my doctorate in English. The similarities were striking: it happened with Alexis de Tocqueville as he travelled throughout New England when the idea of this country was still in its infancy; with Ben Franklin as the Revolutionary War was being fought; with the *Federalist Papers* as the tenets of the Constitution were being debated. It happened with Ralph Waldo Emerson gathering his lectures and essays into books just prior to the Civil War. The list went on and on.

These and other great American thinkers and writers knew that the great experiment of government representation by its people—and not by some power-hungry dictator—was at stake. They all found themselves at crossroads as the *ideal* of America was being defined, questioned, refined, and yes, sometimes reformed.

We are, again, at a crossroads in the history of our nation. The current financial crisis that began in 2007 and in which we are digging ourselves ever deeper is causing us to question many of the ideals we hold dear. Our current president is leading us down the path of socialism—a form of government that controls *every-thing*—not just our healthcare.

More to the point, the "leaders" of our nation have made decisions and signed financial agreements with international financial bodies that may determine the way our very lives are to be handled. They have done this without consulting not only us—the people it most affects—but Congress, the body that is meant to provide oversight in such matters.

These are challenging times for America. We are truly at a watershed moment. Federal budget deficits are beyond being out of control. The government no longer pays attention to the wishes of us, its people, the ones our Founding Fathers fought so hard and so courageously to protect.

We forget that each one of the signers of the Declaration of Independence committed an act of treason against the King of England, punishable by death. One, Thomas McKean of Delaware, wrote John Adams that he was "hunted like a fox by the enemy."[1] He was not alone. They risked everything they held dear to ensure our liberty—our freedom to choose how we live, our right to speak out against our government at any time and for any reason.

That image of a knife through Franklin's throat on the cover isn't just meant to shock, by the way. It's there to help you understand that those in whom we're supposed to trust have instead cut our collective financial throats in order to garner not only gobs and gobs of money but, more insidiously, more power for themselves. Franklin disapproves—just look at his face.

But I digress. In keeping with literary tradition, there has been a deluge of writing about the current catastrophe we're experiencing. Some are more cogent than others. All have helped shed some light on the shadows of what happened with the subprime mortgage scandal. But as I read tract after tract back home in Colorado, I knew there was something missing—connections weren't being made, key information wasn't being presented.

In walks John Truman Wolfe, or rather his essays started appearing in my e-mail inbox. (Franklin would have so loved the Internet, wouldn't he?) From the moment I read his first article, "The Financial Crisis: Behind the Wizards Curtain," I knew here was the "something" I was missing. I knew I had to publish this book and *fast*. It contains vitally important information and, like its predecessors in American history, we are sounding the alarm by publishing these clarion calls.

What follows is simply a collection of articles by a person who felt compelled to chronicle the events as he saw them happening. Wolfe wrote each article, documenting an occurrence in the crisis not knowing that he would be writing the next one. Knowing that some of his readers may not have read the previous article/s, he would often bring some of the prior background information forward to ensure his readers understood the broader context. As you go from article to article, you will witness the story unfold, just as he did—uncovering an agenda by international bankers that is being implemented as I write this.

But Wolfe thoughtfully doesn't just leave us hanging, outraged at what has happened. In the final article, Wolfe provides us with invaluable information on how to preserve our individual financial health. More important, throughout the book he calls for us to act—to make our representative lawmakers stand up to what has happened, to take back control of our finances from those who are stripping it away and put it back into the hands in which is belongs—ours.

What you are about to read will incense you—that I promise. But as Wolfe says towards the end, while there has been a coup, "it is not a *fait accompli*." The power-hungry bankers and politicians think they have won—but they haven't, not yet anyway.

This crisis does not just affect our pocket books. The very ideal of America—the freedoms and liberties we love and all too often take for granted—are being threatened. It is up to each one of us to speak out, to demand that the right actions be taken, so that this historical moment in American history ends as it has done for the past 230-odd years—on the side of freedom and liberty.

My wish is that you read this book in the spirit in which it was written—hard-hitting, eye-opening, provocative. JTW has a favorite saying, "not on my watch." I hope you adopt it as yours.

Patricia Ross, Ph.D.
June 2010

Postscript: While we have worked to include a glossary of financial terms at the bottom of the page on which they appear, this book is full of such. I urge you to use a dictionary liberally. Look up words you don't understand. As Noah Webster, creator of the first American Dictionary said, "There is one remarkable circumstance in our own history which seems to have escaped observation—the mischievous (causing damage) effect of the indefinite application of terms.... Popular errors proceeding from a misunderstanding of words are among the...cause of our political disorders."[2] We have enough "political disorder" right now—don't compound it by not understanding the words you read!

INTRODUCTION

I never wanted to be a banker.

In graduate school, I was captivated by the study of nineteenth-century American history—the era when the promise of free and unexplored land pulled the young republic ever westward to the golden coast. It was the mystery and promise of what was over the next mountain that drew us across the most glorious land imaginable.

So I resisted when my father visited me as I was wrapping up my master's degree and asked, in the most humble manner I had ever heard him speak, if I would drop my plans for a Ph.D. at Berkeley and take over the family home furnishing business—a retail store that was one of the most prominent in the San Francisco Bay Area.

Let me state the problem in the simplest possible terms: the young academic liberal confronting a life as a card-carrying member of the bourgeoisie. Dear God.

So you may be surprised to hear that, after some consideration, I said, "Yes." I said yes for two reasons, neither of which I would recommend as the basis for a happy life.

I felt I owed it to him. I was the oldest son and my two brothers were not interested. How could I let my dad spend his life building a business and not provide a way to let him retire and enjoy his "old age"?

And then there was the financial factor. I was twenty three, had been married two years, and had a one-year-old daughter. I had been living on the pro-verbial graduate student rations of beans and rice, and I was tired of it. The oh-so-capitalist vision of earning a fat paycheck as the heir apparent to a successful Bay-Area furniture brand and playing a lot of golf turned me into a materialist faster than you can say "family country club membership."

It took a few years and some unaccustomed soul searching to wake up to the fact that neither of these motivations aligned with my basic purpose in life, which was to research and write.

The glories of Joseph Walker's trek across the southern Sierra Nevada in the 1830s and selling blue-collar suburbanites the new twenty-three-inch Motorola color TV for 10 percent down and twenty-four equal monthly payments did not fit in the same universe. I taught American history at night down at Oakland Technical High School, the birth-place of the Black Panther Party. This certified me as a gold-seal liberal, but it wasn't enough, and after a few years I left and went looking for a full-time teach-ing job.

After a month of flogging résumés to college administrators who appeared to have been dining on the mind-bending menu of Haight-Ashbury for the previous several years, the family bank account was running on fumes and was beginning to sputter. It was at that point that a friend of a friend told me that Security National Bank—a local retail banking chain—was looking for loan officers.

At this juncture I would have considered a job as a hairdresser in San Francisco, so I rushed down to the bank's headquarters for an interview.

Some may be surprised to learn that the study of the westward movement of the American frontier does not teach one about banking. But working for my dad had done just that. As the assistant controller and credit manager, I dealt with banks and the financing of consumer goods on a daily basis. Additionally, I was under the tutelage of the company's fastidiously demanding controller, who insisted that I balance the company's books literally to the penny every month. So I learned bookkeeping, accounting and financial statements as a matter of hands-on practice. And so I came to the bank with an understanding of credit and finance and the always coveted graduate degree. Even though it was entirely off the subject, it presumably was evidence that my IQ was above roadkill.

Besides, management at SNB were all UC Berkeley guys, and while my degree came from San Jose State, I had done extensive research for my thesis at The Bancroft Library. Situated on the Berkeley campus, Bancroft is one of the finest repositories of Western Americana in the world. So, although I wasn't a full blood brother, I had hunted on the tribe's sacred grounds.

I was hired on the spot.

For reasons that remain unclear to me to this day, I took an instant liking to banking and stormed up the corporate ladder as if someone had slapped a turbo-charger on my career. But my point in all of this is that it was here, immersed in the world of Bay Area banking, that I began using my graduate school research chops to explore the broader subjects of global credit markets, investments, and the oh-so-mysterious universe of the organs of international finance.

PR Spin: How to Move Financial Markets

There were two books that I credit with turning a naïve young banker, a virgin to the world of Wall Street corruption, into a budding financial sleuth.

The first was a book called *The Wall Street Gang*, written by a successful Los Angeles–based money manager named Richard Ney. The text lays bare how "specialists"— those who handle the buy and sell orders of major stocks*—manipulated and controlled the New York Stock Exchange.[1]

The other, with the corny-sounding title of *How to Make the Stock Market Make Money for You*, was written by a man named Ted Warren. Warren uses long-term graphs that show the manipulation of virtually all major stocks and most of the commodities.*[2]

---

* Stock(s)—Short for stock certificate. A document representing the number of shares of a corporation owned by a shareholder.

* Commodities—A commodity is food, metal, or another fixed physical substance that investors buy or sell. For example, corn, gold, currency such as US dollars and Swiss francs, etc.

I didn't take the data in these publications for granted. I tested the theories again and again. Warren's strategies, spelled out in clear, everyday English, worked then and still work today.

More to the point of this introduction, these books provided clear evidence that the major investment markets—stocks and commodities in particular—are controlled. Period.

This, at the time, was a revelation, which has served me well in the ensuing years. Despite well-ingrained illusions to the contrary, things do not just happen in the world of investment and finance. They are caused. Orchestrated by forces unseen by the general public, sophisticated Public Relations campaigns are rolled out via well-connected media networks to spin the strategic messages that flank the campaign *du jour.*

Once I understood that the actions of the investing public were shaped by financial PR machines, I began reading the press with that perspective. In other words, I looked for the underlying intention of the article— what it was trying to get people to do as opposed to the surface message.

It wasn't hard to see this at work. Some years ago, I was following a particular commodity, which appeared to be under accumulation by forces that I felt would drive the price higher. I bought some.

Weeks later, an article appeared in the *Wall Street Journal* saying that an international organization that was in charge of setting the price for this commodity had agreed that the price was not going to exceed a certain level for the foreseeable future. This was just a few cents higher than what I had paid.

The chart of the commodity demonstrated that it was under accumulation by someone/s. My assessment was that they were trying to scare people away from the commodity so they could buy more.

I bought some more—as did, I'm sure, the insiders.

Shortly thereafter, the price of the commodity started to rise. I kept buying as the price went up and the news remained negative or neutral. Several months later, about the time it had tripled, a positive article about the commodity appeared in the *Wall Street Journal*.

Over the next ten days, three more articles appeared in the financial press promoting it as a good investment.

My take now was that the insiders were seeking to increase the number of people buying the commodity so they could sell theirs.

I called my broker. I asked him what his firm's stance was on the commodity. "They just issued a 'buy order'"—meaning they were telling their brokers to recommend it to clients.

"Sell," I said. "All contracts."

The price went up for another few days and then crashed.

Articles in the financial press that promote the buying or selling of an investment product are often not news, but PR spin written with an intention to covertly mold the public's behavior about the investment. This is not an invariable rule, but if you read stories that seem to aggressively promote a particular investment (either positively or negatively) in the mainstream financial media, follow the results into the future. You will often find that the prediction not only missed, but the opposite occurred. Try it.

To be sure, there are exceptions. But these are often young start-up companies that are not traded on major exchanges.

Sometimes the negative PR campaign is designed to take the player all the way out, a lá Lehman Brothers on September 15, 2008, as opposed to driving the price down so it can be purchased for pennies on the dollar, a lá Washington Mutual ten days later.

If you read the books referenced above and start following these things in the media, you'll get sharp at this.

The IMF and the World Bank

This perspective was extremely helpful to me when I started following the activities of the World Bank and the International Monetary Fund (IMF). These are "sister" organizations that were set up at the end of the Second World War essentially to help rebuild war-torn Europe with low-cost loans (the World Bank) and to foster stability in the international currency markets (the IMF).

Despite their altruistic-sounding charters, these two organizations have become nothing less than global financial predators that have turned three-fourths of the planet into debt-ridden junkies.[3]

Sometimes evil is hard to confront. But I tell you without equivocation that the activities of these two international banks have been motivated by a cold, calculated plan to control the populations of Earth.

I know, I know—conspiracy theory and all that. But if you study their trail of financial bondage across the planet, their real intentions become all too clear. And it is not a matter of studying their conduct for a year or two; their strategic plans started decades in the past and run decades into the future.

I started monitoring their activities while working for Security National in the mid-seventies. Some years later, I followed a major currency crisis in Mexico. I found it odd that the IMF had moved in with a multi-billion-dollar "saving" loan. At first, I was interested from a banker's perspective. What had they taken as collateral? I mean, what does an international bank take as security for a loan: oil refineries, mines, government lands? What?

Somehow I got hold of the loan agreement between the IMF and Mexico—a James Bond moment—and I read it. Some of the provisions appeared to have been written by Orwell himself. They granted the IMF control over a wide range of social policies, many of which had no bearing on Mexico's ability to repay the loan.

Something was very odd in the land of many bankers. It was at that point that I started following the activities of the IMF and World Bank more closely as they engaged in an international crime spree that spread economic terrorism around the planet like a fiscal virus.

Having tracked them now for more than three decades, I can tell you that their pattern of operation repeats itself, country to country.

First, they covertly facilitate a currency crisis in the targeted country. This is not difficult to do if one understands that currencies are commodities and can be manipulated on the exchanges on which they trade. It takes capital to do it, but the mechanics are not difficult to put in place. In recent years, people like George Soros have been involved. Think Indonesia, late nineties. Soros and well-placed media outlets push the message about how weak the targeted currency is. Because of this, he is able to sell the currency short* ("betting" it will go down). In this way he drives the value of the currency even lower while making a killing. As the currency crashes, the country experiences growing economic chaos, riots and internal strife.[4]

With the country now trying to participate in international trade and commerce using a currency that has all the attraction of pet food from China, their credit

---

* Sell short—You think a stock/commodity will go down in price. Your broker allows you to borrow these shares of stock. He then sells them at today's high price. You agree to buy them back at a lower price. When the stock goes down to your preset lower price you buy them back. You pocket the difference. You lose if the value of the stock goes up.

rating nose-dives faster than a Nancy Pelosi popularity poll. They can't borrow from traditional sources. Business falters. Unemployment skyrockets. And in some cases, again like Indonesia, riots ensue and blood flows. When the politicians have their colons sufficiently puckered, one or both of the twin sisters of the Apocalypse (the IMF and World Bank) ride in on a white horse.

"Gee, Mr. President. It looks like you're having a problem here. Perhaps we can provide some assistance. Would, say, five or ten billion help to tide you over?"

"Yes, well, the New York bankers have turned their backs on us for no reason at all. This currency issue is temporary, I assure you. How much did you say?"

"Five or ten billion, but we're flexible. Our concern is for the people of your great nation."

"Yes, of course. Who controls how the money is spent?"

"You do, sir."

The President suppresses a smile as he thinks of his private yacht moored in the south of France and his young mistress sunbathing on the foredeck in her topless bikini.

"And what would the terms be?"

"Interest only for the first three years and then we would work out a mutually agreeable repayment plan for the principal. And, of course, you would have to execute our standard loan agreement."

"Certainly. Do you have a copy of that handy?"

One of the bankers pulls a multipage document out

of a Gucci briefcase of shimmering Italian leather and hands it to the President. He begins to scan through it. His brow furrows. He looks up.

"Eh . . . why is there a clause here that mandates how we must educate our young women on matters of family planning and contraception? That has nothing to do with the country's economic strength."

"Well, Mr. President, we feel it does. The population level of the country certainly has a bearing on the nation's prosperity. Wouldn't you agree?"

"I . . . eh, suppose so. But I can't agree to these stipulations regarding our agricultural production or our tax policies. Those are strictly internal matters." The President stands and straightens his back.

The two bankers stand as well. "We're sorry to hear that Mr. President. We were hoping we could help you reduce those unemployment figures." They head for the door. One of them turns, "And Marseille is . . . so beautiful this time of year."

Two weeks later headlines blare: *President Signs $10 Billion IMF Loan Agreement.*

The President puts a cool $500 million in his Swiss bank account. A frenzied pack of federal bureaucrats feast on the balance until only the remains of the bloodied carcass are left for state and local vultures. Perhaps 10 percent will reach the people.

The country will never be able to repay the loan, which, of course, is exactly what the IMF wanted in the first place—control of the country's assets and the ability to dictate social engineering policy.

I know—you think that's a fairy story, an allegory, a fable.

But I have watched this scenario roll out from Moscow to Mexico, from Seoul to Jakarta, for more than thirty years now and this is the drill. The mistress and the dialogue are of course touches of fiction, but the externally *created* currency crisis, economic turmoil, the white horse, the "saving" loan with the Orwellian loan agreements, have been the essence of international banking since the 1970s and perhaps earlier.[5]

Alarm Bells—The GMA

I wrote an article about this in the late nineties but had left the subject alone from a literary perspective since then. It was a statement by the president of the New York Federal Reserve Bank in March 2008 calling for a GMA—a Global Monetary Authority—that set off the alarm bells anew.

A GMA is essentially a planetary financial dictator. And as you likely know, the president of the New York Fed* at that time was none other than Timothy "Pretty Boy" Geithner, the current U.S. Treasury Secretary. So I started a new round of research and writing. Over the next year and a half, I wrote several articles about not only what had happened but, of greater concern, why. They comprise the main body of this book.

---

* New York Fed.—New York branch of the Federal Reserve Bank.

You see, this financial crisis was and is a crisis by design. And there has been a coup d'etat—a hostile takeover—of our financial systems. In order to do anything about it, you first need to know how and why it happened. That is the story of this book.

One of the things that I found in my recent research is that there is an organization behind the IMF and World Bank that is calling the shots, which turns out to be the key puppeteer. Exposing that entity as well as what you can do about this personally to protect yourself and what we need to do as a matter of public policy is the basis of this book.

I hope you enjoy the read. More importantly, I hope the book helps raise your awareness and empowers you to act.

John Truman Wolfe
November 2009

1
The Financial Crisis:
A Look Behind the Wizard's Curtain

March 2009

I'm tired of hearing about subprime mortgages.

It's as if these things were living entities that had spawned an epidemic of economic pornography.

Subprime* mortgages are as much a cause of the current financial chaos as bullets were for the death of JFK.

Someone planned the assassination and someone pulled the trigger.

The media, J. Edgar Hoover and the Warren Commission tried to push Lee Harvey Oswald off on the American public. They didn't buy it.

They shouldn't buy subprime mortgages either. Someone planned the assassination and someone pulled the trigger. Only this time the target is the international financial structure and the bullets are still being fired.

Oh yes, people took out adjustable-rate mortgages they could ill afford which were then sold to Wall Street bankers. The bankers bundled them up like gift

---

* Subprime—non-prime or second chance lending. Borrowers with some late payments or poor credit will get subprime interest rates higher than for prime borrowers.

wrappers at Nordstrom's during the holidays and sold them to other banks after raking off billions in fees. The fees? They were for . . . well . . . they were for wrapping the mortgages in the haute couture of Wall Street.

But it didn't start there. No, no, not by a long shot. So as the late, great Paul Harvey would say, "And now you're going to hear the Rest of the Story."[1]

Are subprime mortgages part of some larger agenda? And if so, what is it?

Stay with me here because Alice is about to slide down the rabbit hole into the looking-glass world of international finance.

"Easy Money" Alan

There are various places we could start this story, but we will begin with the 1987 ascendancy of Rockefeller/Rothschild homeboy Alan Greenspan from the board of directors of J.P. Morgan to the throne of chairman of the Federal Reserve Bank (a position he was to hold for twenty years).

From the beginning of his term as chair, Greenspan was a strong advocate for deregulating the financial services industry: letting the cowboys of Wall Street sow their wild financial oats, so to speak.

He also kept interest rates artificially low, as if he had sprayed the boardroom of the Federal Reserve Bank with some kind of fiscal aspartame.[2]

While aspartame (an artificial sweetener branded as Equal and NutraSweet) keeps the calories down, it has this itty-bitty side effect of converting to formaldehyde in the human body and creating brain lesions.

As we are dealing here with a gruesomely tortured metaphor, let me explain: I am not suggesting that Chairman Greenspan put Equal in his morning coffee, but rather that by his direct influence, interest rates were forced artificially low resulting in an orgy of borrowing and toxic side effects for the entire economy.

The Community Reinvestment Act

Greenspan had been the Fed chairman for seven years when, in 1994, a bill called the Community Reinvestment Act (CRA) was rewritten by Congress. The new version had the purpose of providing loans to help deserving minorities afford homes. Nice thought, but the new legislation opened the door to loans that set aside certain lending criteria: little things like a down payment, enough income to service the mortgage, and a good credit record.[3]

With CRA's facelift, we have in place two of the five elements of the perfect financial storm: Alan (Easy Money) Greenspan at the helm of the Fed and a piece of legislation that turned mortgage lenders into a division of the Salvation Army.

Perhaps you can see the pot beginning to boil here. But the real fuel to the fire was yet to come.

Glass-Steagall

To understand the third element of the storm, we travel back in time to the Great Depression and the 1933 passage of a federal law called the Glass-Steagall Act. As excess speculation by banks was one of the key factors of the banking collapse of 1929, this law forbade commercial banks from underwriting—in other words promoting and selling—stocks and bonds.[4]

That activity was left to the purview of "investment banks" (names of major investment banks you might recognize include Goldman Sachs, Morgan Stanley, and the recently deceased Lehman Brothers).

Commercial banks could take deposits and make loans to people.

Investment banks underwrote stocks and bonds.[*]

To repeat, this law was put in place to prevent the banking speculation that caused the Great Depression. Among other regulations, Glass-Steagall kept commercial banks out of securities.[*5]

Greenspan's role in our not-so-little drama is made clear in one of his first speeches before Congress in 1987 in which he calls for the repeal of the Glass-Steagall Act. In other words, he's trying to get rid of the

---

[*] Investment banks look over a company and then decide to promote the stock; they do due diligence first, of course, but "underwriting" is more of a sales game than anything.

[*] Securities—a certificate of creditorship or property carrying the right to receive interest or dividend, such as shares or bonds.

legislation that kept a lid on banks speculating in financial markets with securities.

He continued to push for the repeal until 1999 when New York banks successfully lobbied Congress to repeal the Glass-Steagall Act. Easy-Money Alan hailed the repeal as a revolution in finance.[6]

Yeah, baby!

A revolution was coming.

With Glass-Steagall gone, and the permissible mergers of commercial banks with investment banks, there was nothing to prevent these combined financial institutions from packaging up the subprime CRA mortgages with normal prime loans and selling them off as mortgage-backed securities through a different arm of the same financial institution. No external due diligence required.[7]

You now have three of the five Horsemen of the Fiscal Apocalypse: Greenspan, CRA mortgages and repeal of Glass-Steagall.

Waiver of Capital Requirements

Enter Hammering Hank Paulson.

In April of 2004, a group of five investment banks met with the regulators at the Securities and Exchange Commission (SEC) and convinced them to waive a rule that required the banks to maintain a certain level of reserves.

This freed up an enormous reservoir of capital, which

the investment banks were able to use to purchase oceans of mortgage-backed securities (cleverly spiked with the subprime CRA loans like a martini in a Bond movie). The banks kept some of these packages for their own portfolios but also sold them by the bucket-load to willing buyers from every corner of the globe.

The investment bank that took the lead in getting the SEC to waive the minimum reserve regulation was Goldman Sachs. The person responsible for securing the waiver was Goldman's chairman, a man named Henry Paulson.[8] With the reserve rule now removed, Paulson became Wall Street's most aggressive player, leveraging the relaxed regulatory environment into a sales and marketing jihad of mortgage-backed securities and similar instruments.

Goldman made billions. And Hammering Hank? According to Forbes magazine, his partnership interest in Goldman in 2006 was worth $632 million. This on top of his $15 million-per-year in annual compensation.[9] Despite his glistening dome, let's say Hank was having a good hair day.

In case this isn't clear, it was Paulson who, more than anyone else on Wall Street, was responsible for the boom in selling the toxic mortgage-backed securities to anyone who could write a check.

Many of you may recognize the name Hank Paulson. It was Paulson who left the Goldman Sachs' chairmanship and came to Washington in mid-2006 as George Bush's Secretary of the Treasury.

And it was Paulson who bludgeoned Congress out of

$700 billion of so-called stimulus money with threats of public riots and financial Armageddon if they did not cough up the dough. He then used $300 billion to "bail out" his Wall Street homeboys to whom he had sold the toxic paper in the first place.[10] All at taxpayer expense.

Makes you feel warm all over, doesn't it?

Congress has its own responsibility for this fiscal madness, but that's another story.

This one still has one more piece—the *pièce de résistance*.

Basel II and the Bank of International Settlements

Greenspan, the Community Reinvestment Act, the repeal of Glass-Steagall, and Paulson getting the SEC to waive the capital rule for investment banks have all set the stage: the economy is screaming along, real estate is in a decade-long boom and the stock market is reaching new highs. Paychecks are fat.

But by the first quarter of 2007, the first nigglings that all was not well in the land of the mortgage-backed securities began to filter into the press. And like a chill whisper rustling through the forest, mentions of rising delinquencies and foreclosures began to be heard.[11]

Still, the stock market continued to rise, with the Dow Jones reaching a high of 14,164 on October 9, 2007. It stayed in the 13,000 range through the month, but in November, a major stock market crash commenced from which we have yet to recover.[12]

It's not just the U.S. stock market that has crashed, however. Stock exchanges around the world have fallen like a rock off a tall building. Most have lost half their value, wiping out countless trillions.[13]

If it were just stock markets that would be bad enough. But, let's be frank; the entire financial structure of the planet has gone into a tailspin and it has yet to hit ground zero.

While there surely would have been losses, truth be told, the U.S. banking system would likely have gotten through this, as would have the rest of the world, had it not been for an accounting rule called Basel II promulgated by the Bank for International Settlements.

Who? What?

That's right, I said an accounting rule.

The final nail in the coffin—and this was really the wooden spike through the heart of the financial markets—was delivered in Basel, Switzerland, at the Bank for International Settlements (BIS).

Never heard of it? Neither have most people; so, let me pull back the wizard's curtain.

Central banks are privately owned financial institutions that govern a country's monetary policy and create that country's money.

The Bank for International Settlements (BIS), located in Basel, Switzerland, is the central banker's bank. There are 55 central banks around the planet that are members, but the BIS is controlled by a board of directors, which is comprised of the elite central bankers of 11 different countries (U.S., UK, Belgium, Canada, France, Germany, Italy, Japan, Switzerland, the Netherlands and Sweden).

Created in 1930, the BIS is owned by its member central banks, which, again, are private entities. The buildings and surroundings that are used for the purpose of the bank are inviolable. No agent of the Swiss public authorities may enter the premises without the express consent of the bank. The bank exercises supervision and police power over its premises. The bank enjoys immunity from criminal and administrative jurisdiction.

In short, they are above the law.

This is the ultra-secret world of the planet's central bankers and the top of the food chain in international finance. The board members fly into Switzerland for once-a-month meetings, which they hold in secret.

In 1988 the BIS issued a set of recommendations on how much capital commercial banks should have. This standard, referred to as Basel I, was adopted worldwide.

In January of 2004 our boys got together again and issued new rules about the capitalization of banks (for those that are not fluent in bank-speak, this is essentially what the bank has in reserves to protect itself and its depositors).

This was called Basel II.

Within Basel II was an accounting rule that required banks to adjust the value of their marketable securities (such as mortgage-backed securities) to the "market price" of the security. This is called mark to market. There can be some rationality to this in certain circumstances, but here's what happened.

The Media and Mark to Market

As news and rumors began to circulate about some of the subprime CRA loans in the packages of mortgage-backed securities, the press, always at the ready to forward the most salacious and destructive information available, started promoting these problems.[14]

As a result, the value of these securities fell. And when one particular bank did seek to sell some of these securities, they got bargain-basement prices.

Instantly, per Basel II, that meant that the hundreds of billions of dollars of these securities being held by banks around the world had to be marked down— marked to the market.[15]

It didn't matter that the vast majority of the loans (90 percent plus) in these portfolios were paying on time.[16] If, say, Lehman Brothers had gotten firesale prices for their mortgage-backed securities, the other banks, which held these assets on their books, now had to mark to market, driving their financial statements into the toilet.

Again, it didn't matter that the banks were receiving payments (cash flow) from their loan portfolios; the value of the package of loans had to be written down.

A rough example would be if the houses on your

street were all worth about $400,000. You owe $300,000 on your place and so have $100,000 in equity. Your neighbor, Bill, in selling his house, uncovered a massive invasion of termites. He had to sell the house in a hurry and wound up with $200,000, half the real value.

Shortly thereafter, you get a demand letter from your bank for $100,000 because your house is only worth $200,000 according to "the market." Your house doesn't have termites, or perhaps just a few. Doesn't matter.

Of course, if the value of your home goes below the loan value, banks can't make you cough up the difference.

But if you are a bank, Basel II says you must adjust the value of your mortgage-backed securities if another bank sold for less—termites or no.

When the value of their assets was marked down, it dramatically reduced their capital (reserves), and this—*their capital*—*determined the amount of loans they could make.*

The result? Banks couldn't lend. The credit markets froze.

Someone recently said that credit was the life blood of the economy.[17]

This happens to be a lie. Hard work, production, and the creation of products that are needed and wanted by others—these are the true life blood of an economy.

But, let's be honest, credit does drive much of the current U.S. economy: home mortgages, auto loans and Visas in more flavors than a Baskin-Robbins store.

That is, until the banks had to mark to market and turn the IV off.

The Crisis

With mark to market, mortgage lending slammed to a halt as if it had run headlong into a cement wall, credit lines were canceled, and credit card limits were reduced and in some cases eliminated altogether.[18] In short, with their balance sheets butchered by Basel II, banks were themselves going under and those that weren't simply stopped lending. The results were like something from a financial horror film—if there were such a thing.

Prof. Peter Spencer, one of Britain's leading economists, makes it very clear that the Basel II regulations "...are at the root cause of the crunch..." and that "...if the authorities retain the strict Basel regulations, the full scale of the eventual credit crunch and economic slump could be disastrous."

"The consequences for the macro-economy," he says "of not relaxing [the Basel regulations] are unthinkable."[19]

Spencer isn't the only one who sees this. There have been calls in both the U.S. and abroad to, at least, relax Basel II until the crisis is over. But the Boys from Basel haven't budged an inch. The U.S. did modify these rules somewhat a year after the devastation had taken place here, but the rules are still fully in place in the rest of the world and the results are appalling.

The credit crisis that started in the U.S. has spread around the globe with the speed that only the digital universe could make possible. You'd think Mr. Freeze from the 1997 Batman & Robin movie was doing his thing.

We have already noted that stock markets around the world have lost half of their value, erasing trillions. Some selected planet-wide stats make it clear that it is not just stock values that have crashed.

As of this writing, China's industrial production fell 12 percent last year, while Japan's exports to China fell 45 percent and Taiwan's were off 55 percent. South Korea's overseas shipments decreased 17 percent, while their economy shrank 5.6 percent.

Singapore's exports were off the most in thirty-three years and Hong Kong's exports plunged the most in fifty years.

Germany had a 7.3 percent decline in exports in the fourth quarter of last year, while Great Britain's real estate market declined 18 percent in the last quarter compared to a year earlier.

Australia's manufacturing contracted at a record pace last month, bringing the index to the lowest level on record.[20]

There's much more, but I think it is obvious that the "credit pipe" can no longer be smoked.

Welcome to planetary cold turkey.

Oddities

It is fascinating to look at the date coincidence of the crash in the U.S. Earlier I noted that the stock market continued to rise throughout 2007, peaking in October of 2007. The dip in October turned to a rout in November.

The Basel II standards were implemented here by the U.S. Financial Accounting Standards on November 15, 2007.

There are more oddities.

Despite the fact that Hammering Hank dished out hundreds of billions to his banker buddies to "stimulate" the economy and defrost the credit markets, the recipients of these taxpayer bailout billions have made it clear that they will be reducing the amount of money they will be lending over the next eighteen months by as much as $2 trillion to conform to Basel II.

What do you think—Hank, with his Harvard MBA, didn't know? The former chairman of the most successful investment bank in the world didn't know that the Basel II regulations would inhibit his homies from turning the lending back on?

Maybe it slipped his mind.

Like the provision he put into his magnum opus, the $700 billion bailout called TARP. It carried a provision for the Federal Reserve to start paying interest on the money banks deposited with it.[21]

Think this through for a minute. The apparent problem is that the credit markets are frozen. Banks aren't lending. They can't use the money from TARP to lend because Basel II says they can't. On top of this, Paulson's bailout lets the Fed pay interest on funds banks deposit there.

If I am the president of a bank, and let's say that I'm not Basel II impaired, why in the world am I going to lend to customers in the midst of the worst financial crisis in human history when I can click a mouse and deposit my funds with the Fed and sit back and earn interest from them until the chaos subsides?

But, hey, maybe Hank's been putting aspartame in his coffee.

No, this stuff is as obvious as the neon signs on Broadway to the folks who play this game. This is banking 101.

So, given the provisions of Basel II and the refusal of the BIS to lift or suspend the regulations when they are clearly the driving force behind the planet-wide credit crisis, and considering the lack of provisions in Paulson's bailout bill to mandate that taxpayer funds given to banks must actually be lent, and given the added incentive in the bill for banks to deposit their bread with the Fed, one gets the idea that maybe, just maybe, these programs weren't designed to cure this crisis; maybe they were designed to create it.

Indeed, my friends, this is crisis by design.

Someone planned the assassination, and someone pulled the trigger.

The Rubber Meets the Road

All of which begs the question, how come?

Why drive the planet into the throes of fiscal withdrawal—of job losses, vaporized home equity, and pillaged 401ks and IRAs*?

Because when the pain is bad enough, when the stock markets are in shambles, when the cities are teaming with the unemployed, when the streets are awash with riots, when governments are drenched in the sweat of eviction and overthrow, then the doctor will come with the needle of International Financial Control.

This string of ineffective solutions put forth by people who know better are convincing bankers, investors, corporations and governments of one thing: the system failed and even the U.S. government—the anchor of international finance which is blamed for causing the disaster—has lost its credibility.

The purpose of this financial crisis is to take down the United States and the U.S. dollar as the stable datum of planetary finance and, in the midst of the resulting confusion, put in its place a Global Monetary Authority—a planetary financial control organization to "ensure this never happens again."

Sound Orwellian? Sound conspiratorial? Sound too evil or too vast to be real?

This entity is being moved forward by world leaders

---

* 401K and IRA's—Savings set aside usually for retirement. Often put into stocks and bonds to allow them to grow in value over the working years.

"as we speak." It is coming and the pace is quickening.

A year ago, I saw an article in which the president of the New York Federal Reserve Bank was calling for a "Global Monetary Authority," or GMA, to deal with the world's financial crisis. While I have been following international banking institutions for some time, this was the clue that they were making their move.[22] I wrote an article on it at the time.

By the way, as some may recall, the president of the New York Fed last year was a man named Timothy Geithner. Geithner was very involved in structuring the booby-trapped TARP bailout with Paulson and Bernanke.[23] Of course, now, he is the Secretary of the Treasury of the United States.

Change we can believe in.

Once Geithner started to push a global financial authority as the solution to the world's financial troubles, other world leaders and opinion-leading voices in international finance began to forward this message. It has been a PR campaign of growing intensity. Meanwhile, behind the scenes, the international bankers are keeping their hands on the throat of the credit markets, choking off lending while the planet's financial markets asphyxiate and become more and more desperate for a solution.

British Prime Minister Gordon Brown, who has taken the point on this, has said that the world needs a "new Bretton Woods."[24] This is the positioning for the GMA. (Bretton Woods, New Hampshire, was the location where world leaders met after the Second

World War and established the international financial organizations called the International Monetary Fund [IMF] and the World Bank to help provide lending to countries in need after the war.[25])

Sir Evelyn de Rothschild called for improved (international) regulations,[26] while the managing director of the IMF suggested a "high level council of ministers capable of reaching agreements and implementing them."[27]

The former director of the IMF, Michael Camdessus, called on "the global village" to "urgently and radically" implement international regulations.[28]

As the crisis has intensified, so too have calls for a global financial policeman; and, of late, the PR has been directed in favor of—surprise—the Bank for International Settlements.

The person at the BIS who was primarily responsible for the creation of Basle II is Jaime Caruana. The BIS board has now appointed him as the general manager, the bank's chief executive position, where he will be in charge of dealing with the current financial crisis, which he had no small part in creating.[29]

A few well-chosen sound bites tell the story. Following a recent IMF function, discussion centered on the fact that the BIS could provide effective market regulation, while the *Global Investor* magazine opined that "perhaps the Bank of International Settlements in Basel" could undertake the task of best dealing with the crisis in the financial markets.

The UK *Telegraph* is right out front with it:

Global financial crisis: does the world need a new banking 'policeman'?

....A new global solution is needed because the machinery of global economic governance barely exists...it's time for a Bretton Woods for this century.

The big question is whether it is time to establish a global economic "policeman" to ensure the crash of 2008 can never be repeated....

The answer might be staring us in the face in the form of the Bank for International Settlements (BIS). The BIS has been spot on throughout this.[30]

And so you see, this was a drill. This was a strategy: Bring in Easy Money Alan to loosen the credit screws; open the floodgates to mortgage loans to the seriously unqualified with the CRA; bundle these as securities; repeal Glass-Steagall and waive capital requirements for investment banks so the mortgage-backed securities could be sold far and wide; wait until the loans matured a bit and some became delinquent, and ensure the media spread this news as if Heidi Fleiss had had a sex-change operation; then slam in an international accounting rule that was guaranteed to choke off all credit and crash the leading economies of the world.

Ensure the right people were in the key places at

the right time—Greenspan, Paulson, Geithner and Caruana.

When the economic pain was bad enough, promote the theory that the existing financial structures did not work and that a Global Monetary Authority—a "Bretton Woods for the twenty-first century"—was needed to solve the crisis and ensure this does not happen again.

Which is exactly where we are right now.

What Do You Do?

Let me preface this section by saying that this is advice designed to help you orient your assets—i.e., your reserves, your retirement plans, etc.—to the Brave New World of international finance. It is not meant as advice about what you do with your business, or your job, or your personal life.

Those things are all senior to this subject, which has a very narrow focus. There is an embarrassment of riches of materials that you can use to stay ahead of and on top of this crisis. Use them to flourish and prosper. This article is not a call to cut back or contract. It is to provide you information so you know what is going on and can plan.

Enough said.

First of all, while not likely, but just in case Timothy Geithner is shocked into some New Age epiphany and Ben Bernanke grows some real wisdom in his polished dome, this is what the government should do:

1. Cancel any aspects of Basel II that are causing banks to misevaluate their assets.

2. Remove the provision of TARP that permits the Fed to pay interest on deposits.

3. Mandate that any funds given under the TARP bailout or that are to be given to banks in the future must be used to lend to deserving borrowers.

4. Repeal the Community Reinvestment Act.

5. Reinstate Glass-Steagall.

6. Restore mandated capital requirements to investment banks.

7. And in case Congress decides to cease being a flock of frightened sheep and take responsibility for the country's monetary policy, they should get rid of the privately owned Federal Reserve Bank and establish a monetary system based on production and property.

8. But if a global monetary authority is put in place, it should not be controlled by central bankers. It should be fully controlled directly by governments with real oversight over it and with a system of checks and balances. This you can communicate when this matter hits Congress or the White House or both (which it almost certainly will).

And what do you do with your reserves in this Brave New World of international finance?

Modesty aside, please do what I have been recommending for a few years now: get liquid (out of the stock and bond markets) and put some of your assets into precious metals, gold and silver, but more heavily into silver.

Keep the rest in cash (CDs and T-bills) and perhaps a small bit in some stronger foreign currencies like the Swiss franc or Chinese yuan (also referred to as the RMB, which is short for renminbi).

And remember that my recommendations are based on my thirty years of experience in banking, finance, and investments, but I have no crystal ball and make no guarantees regarding my recommendations.

We are living in the most challenging economic times this planet has ever seen. I hope this article has helped shed some light on what is currently happening on the international financial scene. I didn't cover everything or everyone involved, but these are the broad strokes.

If you want to follow these shenanigans, log on to The Road to London Summit (http://www.london-summit. gov.uk/en/). It will all look and sound very reasonable—all about saving jobs and homes—but you have seen behind the wizard's curtain, and the above is what is really going on.

Keep your powder dry.

2
Hitler's Bank Goes Global

May 2009

Publisher's Note: *This is the article that notes the date of the coup with the creation of the Financial Stability Board (FSB). The FSB is the global monetary authority Wolfe noted in Chapter One. On April 2, 2009, when the G-20* signed the communiqué from the BIS in Basel, the FSB was born. It marks the date that Big Banker effected the hostile takeover of global finances, including the takeover of the American economy.*

A towering citadel housing what is essentially a sovereign state known as the Bank for International Settlements is located in Basel, Switzerland. The bank now controls the financial affairs of planet Earth.

If you think this is an exaggeration or the conspiratorial ramblings of the author...or not, I invite you to read on.

---

* G-20—A group of twenty (G-20) Finance Ministers and Central Bank Governors, established in 1999.

The Purpose of the Financial Crisis

I wrote the first installment of this article—"The Financial Crisis: A Look Behind the Wizard's Curtain"—in mid-March of this year.

The article included the following statement:

"The purpose of this financial crisis is to take down the United States and the U.S. dollar as the stable datum of planetary finance and, in the midst of the resulting confusion, put in its place a global monetary authority—a planetary financial control organization 'to ensure this never happens again.'"

This purpose has now been accomplished.

The dollar, the former king of currencies, now goes begging in the pant-suited persona of Hillary Clinton to our creditors at the Chinese Communist Party.[1]

Almost unthinkable a few short years ago, the U.S. dollar is fast losing its status as the world reserve currency, and any thought of saving it is being nuked by the Bernanke, Geithner, and Summers commitment to their Alice-in-Wonderland trillion-dollar budget deficits.

I would not be surprised to see central banks start using the renminbi (the currency of the newly awakened People's Republic of China—also called the yuan) for international trade and reserves in the not too distant future. This prediction will likely be scoffed at by global economists, but then they have about as much credibility as Larry, Moe and Curly these days.

A more generally discussed alternative is the

International Monetary Fund's SDR (which stands for Special Drawing Rights). There is no production or property behind the SDR. It is one of those clown currencies that are made up out of thin air—a magic trick central bankers like to do. Intoxicated by the power of the purse, they think of themselves as fiscal alchemists.

But the dollar has seen its glory. It can return one day, if Washington ever finds its financial backbone. But let's be real, with the exception of a very few, like Ron Paul in the House and Tom Coburn in the Senate, these folks are addicted to spending like junkies on horse.

More importantly, the other shoe has dropped. Like some ghoulish predator from another *Alien* sequel, a Global Monetary Authority has been born. It lives.

The Financial Stability Board

On April 2, 2009, the members of the G-20 (a loose-knit organization of the central bankers and finance ministers of the 20 major industrialized nations) issued a communiqué that gave birth to what is no less than Big Brother in a three-piece suit.[2]

Which means? . . .

The communiqué announced the creation of the all-too-Soviet-sounding Financial Stability Board (FSB)—and no, I'm not going to make a crack about the fact that this acronym is the same as that of the Russian intelligence service that replaced the KGB.

The Financial Stability Board. Remember that name well, because they now have control of the planet's finances . . . and, when one peels the onion of the communiqué, control of much, much more.

The FSB morphed into existence from an earlier incarnation called the Financial Stability Forum. The Financial Stability Forum (FSF) was established in 1999 to promote international financial stability through co-operation in financial supervision and surveillance. Since it had done such a wonderful job, the central bankers decided to expand its powers and give it a new name.[3]

A *board* sounds like it has more authority than a *forum.* But the name change isn't the problem. The FSB's broadened mandate includes, under point five:

> As obligations of membership, member countries and territories commit to pursue the maintenance of financial stability, maintain the openness and transparency of the financial sector, implement international financial standards (including the twelve key International Standards and Codes), and agree to undergo periodic peer reviews, using among other evidence IMF/World Bank public Financial Sector Assessment Program reports.[4]

Rather a mouthful of elitist banker-speak. But, as a friend of mine is fond of saying, "The devil is in the details."

The Twelve International Standards and Codes

While several press releases from the G-20's London conclave reference these codes as though they were handed down from a fiscal Mount Sinai, finding the specifics takes some digging.

But then the Bank for International Settlements (BIS), out of which the FSB operates, has never seen transparency as one of its core values. In fact, given its fascist pedigree, transparency hasn't been a value at all. Known as Hitler's bank, the Bank for International Settlements worked arm in arm with the Nazis, facilitating the transfer of gold from Nazi-occupied countries to the Reichsbank, and kept their lines open to the international financial community during the Second World War.[5]

As noted in the first article, the BIS is completely above the law.

It is like a sovereign state. Its personnel have diplomatic immunity for their persons and papers. No taxes are levied on the bank or the personnels' salaries. The grounds are sovereign, as are the buildings and offices. The Swiss government has no legal jurisdiction over the bank and no government agency or authority has oversight over its operations.

In a 2003 article titled "Controlling the World's Monetary System: The Bank for International Settlements," Joan Veon wrote:

The BIS is where all of the world's central banks

meet to analyze the global economy and determine what course of action they will take next to put more money in their pockets, since they control the amount of money in circulation and how much interest they are going to charge governments and banks for borrowing from them. . . .
When you understand that the BIS pulls the strings of the world's monetary system, you then understand that they have the ability to create a financial boom or bust in a country. If that country is not doing what the money lenders want, then all they have to do is sell its currency.[6]

And if you don't find that troubling, a close reading of the new powers of the FSB are chilling.

The twelve key International Standards and Codes, which are minimum requirements, contain such things as:

- clear specification of the structure and functions of government;

- statistical and data gathering from ministries of education, health, finance and other agencies;

- corporate governance principles;

- shareholder rights;

- personal savings;

- secure retirement incomes;

- international accounting standards to be observed in the preparation of financial statements;

- international standards of auditing;

- securities settlement;

- foreign exchange settlement;

- minimal capital adequacy for banks;

- risk management;

- ratification and implementation of UN instruments; and

- criminalizing the financing of terrorism.

"Sounds oppressive," you say. "But I don't really care what a bunch of bankers do in Basel, Switzerland. It's got nothing to do with me." However, I am writing this to tell you that it has everything to do with you, your family, your business, your country, and—if you're up to it—your planet.

Because as currently structured, the dictates of the Financial Stability Board will impact your life without any say-so on your part whatsoever. Here's one example from an article written by former Clinton advisor and political strategist Dick Morris in an article for *The Bulletin* on April 6, 2009.

> The FSB is also charged with "implementing...
> tough new principles on pay and compensation
> and to support sustainable compensation schemes
> and the corporate social responsibility of all firms."

That means that the FSB will regulate how much executives are to be paid and will enforce its idea of corporate social responsibility at "all firms."[7]

You begin to see what's involved here.

You see, these standards and codes are commitments, obligations, and requirements, not merely advice. The strategy, policies, and regulations of the FSB are worked out at the senior levels of the bank. They are approved by the plenary (the members of a body collectively) and implemented through the national representatives.

The Structure

The plenary, in this sense, is the complete membership body of the FSB. And the membership, my friends— the national representatives who implement these policies— just happen to be the heads of the planet's most powerful central banks. And in case it slipped your mind, most central banks are private institutions and answerable to no one.

Take our central bank, the Federal Reserve Bank. Yes, the chairman is appointed by the President and often testifies before Congress, but there is virtually no public control over the institution. It can't be audited nor can Congress tell it what to do. It is not really accountable to anyone.[8] The idea that the Fed is a government agency subject to the control of Congress is a PR line. It is simply not true.

Among other things, central banks govern a country's monetary policy and create (print) the country's money. They make income by charging interest on the money they loan to the government.

Watch this, because if you blink, you'll miss it. Governments are perpetually in debt. They are always borrowing money. They have a mental disorder that prevents them from spending less than they collect in taxes—BDD, Budget Deficit Disorder. And if it looks like they might balance the books some year, why, someone can always start a war.

Here's an example.

Let's say the annual budget calls for the U.S. government to spend $2.5 trillion. But the income will only be $2 trillion. They're going to be a little short. But no worries, they have the ultimate credit card—a debt limit that they themselves control. If they borrow up to the established limit, they can just vote it higher—which they have done to the tune of a cool $11.2 trillion dollars.

The Fed loves this.

Listen as the Secretary of the Treasury calls the chairman of the Fed.

"Ben. It's Tim."

"Dude. What's happening?"

"I need a little bread. Friggin' Taliban again."

"No problem, Timbo. How much you looking for?"

"Five hundred big ones."

Ben licks his lips. "Anything for you, big guy. Send me the notes and I'm down with the five hundred. Five percent work for you?"

"Whatever."

So the Treasury prints up $500 billion dollars' worth of IOUs—they are called Treasury bills (short term), notes (medium term) or bonds (long term)—and sends them over to the Fed with a fifth of Chivas.

In the old days, the Fed would print the cash. These days, they click a mouse.

Now here's the part where you aren't allowed to blink. When the Fed prints the money or clicks the mouse, they have no money themselves. They are just creating it out of thin air. They just print it, or send it digitally. And then they charge interest on the money they lent to the Treasury. A hundred-dollar bill costs $0.04 to print. But the interest is charged on the $100. Go ahead: read it again; the words won't change.

The interest on the national debt last year (2008) was $451,154,049,950.63.[9] That's $1.23 billion a day. These are the same people that are now running our banks, insurance companies and automobile manufacturers.

But I digress.

Sure, I oversimplified it. The Fed doesn't own all the debt and they do some other things. But these are the basics. That is how a central bank works.

It is the heads of the planet's central banks and some

finance ministers that make up the membership of the FSB.

In brief, here's how it works: the Board's leadership provides strategies, policies and regulations to the membership. The members vote on the matters and then see to their implementation in their respective countries.

FSB leadership is in the hands of the chairman, Mario Draghi. Mr. Draghi is also the governor of Italy's central bank. He is a former executive director of the World Bank and like his comrade in international finance Henry Paulson—the former U.S. Secretary of the Treasury who bludgeoned Congress out of the first $700 billion bailout package—Draghi was a managing director of Goldman Sachs until 2006. Like Paulson, he left Goldman in 2006, a year before the financial crisis exploded: Paulson went to Washington to run the U.S. Treasury; Draghi went to Rome to run Italy's financial system as well as the Financial Stability Forum (forerunner to the Financial Stability Board).

Let's call it government by Goldman, shall we?

The Real Situation

More to the point, you may have noticed that you weren't consulted on this setup. Neither was Congress. In other words, the command channel for implementing global financial strategies goes from the FSB leadership to its central banker members and from them to the world's financial institutions. You don't get a peek, neither does Congress, nor, for that matter, does the White House.[10]

And while there may be some accountability in some of the member countries, by and large these central-bankers have the authority to implement these regulations and strategies. And they are held responsible by the FSB to do so.

In short, on April 2, 2009, the President signed a communiqué that essentially turns over financial control of the country, and the planet, to a handful of central bankers, who, besides dictating policy covering everything from your retirement income to shareholder rights, will additionally have access to your health and education records.

There is also this troubling little line about "*clear specification of the structure and functions of government.*"

There is no oversight here. Not by you, not by Congress, not by anybody. No oversight over a handful of central bankers who operate out of a clandestine organization that is above the law and is responsible for having implemented and enforced the "standards" that froze world credit markets and precipitated the worst financial crisis in the planet's history (see "The Financial Crisis: A Look Behind the Wizard's Curtain").

This is nothing short of a full-blown *coup d'état*— a takeover of the world's financial systems. There were no wild-eyed revolutionaries brandishing A-K 47s or machetes stained with the blood of the status quo.

The coup was accomplished with the feigned civility of Armani-clad politicians in polished mahogany conference rooms turning their countries' financial autonomy over to a cabal of bankers in Basel, Switzerland with the stroke of a pen.

I haven't heard word one out of Congress about this, but I'm afraid they are a few clowns short of a circus up there.

Which begs the question, what the hell do we do about this?

The Solution

There are two critical things that need to be done.

The first lies in the fact that the communiqué signed by the President is an agreement that is binding on the United States and, as such, requires approval by Congress. If classed as a *treaty*, it requires approval by two-thirds of the Senate. At the very least, approval should be by *congressional-executive agreement*, which requires a majority of both houses of Congress.[11]

The agreement signed in London on April 2, 2009, has been called a New Bretton Woods (Bretton Woods being the location of a meeting of world leaders toward the end of the Second World War, which gave birth to the international financial organizations the World Bank and the International Monetary Fund). The original Bretton Woods agreement was put in place as a congressional-executive agreement.[12] So this "new

Bretton Woods" should at least do the same.

This step is just to get Congress to recognize their responsibility here. The Federal Reserve Act, the bill that established the Federal Reserve System, was passed in 1913 two nights before Christmas by a sparsely attended Congress.

People have been complaining about this ever since. What do you say we don't let this happen again? Not on our watch. Congress needs to understand that it has a responsibility to approve any agreement signed by the President that is binding on this nation.

But the point is not to just get Congress to approve what has been done. It is to first get them to recognize that agreements have been made that affect our entire financial system, that it is their responsibility to shape these agreements in a way that is beneficial to our Republic, *and* to provide a mechanism for real oversight of this international body.

Central bankers should not be making decisions about international finance without oversight and a system of checks and balances that are reflective of those provided by a republican form of government.

I am, of course, not talking about a political party here. No, no. I'm talking about the American form of government where citizens elect others to represent them.

A republican form of government is one that is operated by representatives chosen by the people.

Congress must step up to the plate. They must insist that the Financial Stability Board be ratified either by treaty or congressional-executive agreement. And that ratification must include the creation of a body with oversight and corrective powers that is comprised of representatives of all the nations involved who are chosen from each country's elected officials.

There is nothing inherently evil about an international financial organization. As much as we might protest it, it is a global world today, and a body that oversees the smooth flow and interchange of currencies and other financial instruments is needed in today's world.

But the organization cannot be controlled by international bankers who are not answerable to the citizens of the countries in which they operate. It should be overseen by a senior level group which itself is organized as a liberal republic, following the original model of the United States.

Why? Because the system of government originally created by the United States has been the most successful form of government in man's history. Any problems with the system have come about as a result of deviations from the original structure—a representative form of government with adequate checks and balances.

Such a body could help create an international economic system in which those that want to be successful can be so. It would also allow them to take an active role in controlling their futures by effectively participating in the legislative process.

ACT!

Let your representatives and senators know: the Financial Stability Board must be approved by Congress and must be subject to oversight by elected officials of the countries involved.

Personal visits, followed by calls and faxes to both Washington and local offices, are the most effective. Don't be surprised if they don't know what you're talking about. Politely insist they find out and take action. And understand this when dealing with legislators or their staffs: they are focused almost exclusively on legislation that has already been introduced—a bill with a number on it.

That is not the case here. You want them to take action on this matter by introducing legislation that brings the approval and structure of the Financial Stability Board under congressional control.

This can be accomplished.

"All tyranny needs to gain a foothold is for people of good conscience to remain silent."

—Thomas Jefferson

Find your elected officials here: http://www.visi.com/juan/congress/

And let them know what they need to do. After all, they work for you.

3
The Financial Crisis:
The Hidden Beginning

June 2009

Publisher's Note: *This article was written three months after the original article,* "Behind the Wizard's Curtain." *As Wolfe continued to do his research on the global crisis, he realized that there was an earlier beginning to the story than what he had presented in the first article. What follows is an account of what the events that led up to the first Basel Accord, Basel I.*

On April 2, 2009, control of the planet's banks was turned over to the secret decisions of eleven men—board members of a Swiss organization with a troubling Nazi past.

Banking wasn't always that way. . . .

My secretary would come into my office every morning at 9:00 a.m. with a room-service smile and an armload of computer printouts.

She would place the reports on my desk as if she were serving a fine meal and arrange them just so, with the overdraft report (OD) on top, and then slip out of the office as if she were trying not to wake anyone.

The customer's name was on the left side of the page followed by the date the account was opened, the six-month average balance, and a listing of the offending checks that had sentenced the account to the OD report. The amount of the checks and the total overdraft were featured prominently on the right-hand side of the page like perps in a police lineup.

The decisions were twofold: do I pay the checks and, whether paid or not, do I assess overdraft charges? Over-draft charges have gotten rapacious in recent years, but they were $4.00 an item back then, and believe it or not, it takes time, money and effort for bank personnel to track down the impostor and send it home branded with banking's scarlet letter—*insufficient funds*.

I would usually let the charges stand, but I was not a tough close if someone called in with a plausible story on why the check beat the deposit to their account. This was usually good for one round of reversed OD charges, but rarely repeated despite screenplay-quality presentations.

A friend of mine had a leather shop down the street where he handcrafted sandals, belts and wallets adorned with peace symbols, which, in those days, were found on everything from condoms to dog collars. He was of the genus *Hippy*, drove a ratty VW van covered in flowery orange and yellows, and wore iconic bell-bottomed Levi's. There was great profit in leather goods, but Jimmy paid no attention to his bank balance and overdrew the account with such regularity I sometimes wondered if he was trying to ensure the branch remained profitable.

Banking was more personal then: "Jimmy, you're OD again."

"That's bullshit, man."

"No, Jimmy. It's not bullshit. You're overdrawn $312."

"I can't be overdrawn. I just gave you guys a bunch of bread. You probably held it so some checks would come in first and you could hit me with a bunch of overdraft charges."

"Lay off the weed, Jimmy. When did you make the deposit?"

"Yesterday. Seven hundred bones. Gave it to that foxy black chick with the Afro."

"Yes. I see it. But you're still OD."

"You're bummin' me out, man, really bummin' me out."

"When was the last time you reconciled your account, Jimmy?"

"Don't put that on me, man. That form is a bad trip. Gives me a migraine."

"Bring your last three statements down to the branch, and I'll have bookkeeping reconcile the account for you."

"Groovy. You gonna reverse the OD charges?"

"Not a prayer. Bring $312 with you."

"Fascist."

Your local bank was also where you went to get a loan to buy your new home. And there it stayed until it was paid off.

A customer would come into the branch, fill out an

application and, if approved, we would finance 75–80 percent of the purchase. The borrower would come up with the balance. When the loan was approved, we would issue the funds to escrow at the appropriate time and put the loan on our books, where it would stay, earning the bank the going rate of interest for home loans.

I'm sure there are still some community banks that offer personal service instead of having you talk to someone in the Philippines about your credit card, but I wrote this to make the point that banking—and mortgage banking in particular—has changed.

Banks started selling loans to investors while keeping the servicing. In other words, the borrower would keep making his mortgage payments to the bank that made the loan but the payment would be sent on to the investor who had purchased the loan from the bank. The investors were usually pension plans or large investment funds.

But this change in mortgage lending was just beginning. A group of leading bankers would soon turn mortgage banking into a cancer that would eat the industry alive. What follows is the earlier beginning to our story, "The Financial Crisis: A Look Behind the Wizard's Curtain"—a chronicle of the men and institutions who designed the current crisis: a crisis by design.

The Japanese

It was 1985, and the Land of the Rising Sun had become the planet's largest creditor nation.* Words like *Toyota*, *Panasonic*, and *Yamaha* had become part of the lexicon in places such as Omaha, Cleveland, and Des Moines. In 1970, the ten largest banks in the world were American. By the end of the eighties, six of the ten largest banks in the world were Japanese.

What happened?

The Japanese banks were pampered and protected by their government like corporate rock stars. They were permitted to operate with small amounts of reserve capital, which gave them an advantage over other banks and enabled them to expand their market share at the expense of their competition—the major money-center banks in New York and London represented by the dual-headed Darth Vaders of international finance, the U.S. Federal Reserve Bank and the Bank of England.[1]

The Gunfight at the O.K. Corral had nothing on what was about to occur to the banking samurai of Tokyo.

In the eighties, governments had varying regulations about how much capital their banks had to maintain. These standards were supposed to ensure that banks had enough in reserves to protect themselves and their depositors against bad loans.

---

* Creditor nation—When a country exports more than it imports, it has a balance of payments surplus. When it imports more than it exports it becomes a debtor nation.

These "capital adequacy standards" were set as a percentage of the bank's assets. In other words, if the capital requirements were 8 percent and a bank had $8,000,000 in capital, they could expand their balance sheet to $100,000,000 in assets (loans and other investments).

But let's say the capital requirements were 4 percent. Taking the same bank with the same $8,000,000 in capital, they could carry $200,000,000 in loans and other assets, generating a great deal more income and profit for the bank.

If the capital requirements were 10 percent, that same bank could have assets of $80,000,000—fewer loans, less income.

You get the picture: the capital requirements dictated what amount of assets the bank could carry. And the amount of assets determined how much income the bank could generate.

The Japanese banks had low capital requirements—one central banker reported them to be as low as 3 percent. Others claimed 6 percent.[2] But in either case, they were low. The low capital requirements enabled them to hold more assets, which in turn spun off more income. The elevated income enabled them to offer lower interest rates on loans than the competition could. Their market share grew.

In time, Japanese banking became the Godzilla of international finance—a condition that did not sit well with Alan Greenspan, the recently appointed chairman of the Federal Reserve Bank, who dealt with the

matter like a Mafia chieftain whose turf had been vio-
lated by the yakuza.

As soon as he assumed the throne at the Fed, Greenspan, complaining about advantage enjoyed by the
Japanese banks, went to his comrades in coin at the
Bank of England and executed a two-party agreement establishing capital adequacy standards for U.S.
and UK banks.[3] The two of them then turned on their
pinstriped Nipponese brothers and told them that
they were going to be excluded from Western markets
unless they agreed to an international standard of capital adequacy.

The Japanese, dragged to the agreement like a dog
to a bath, signed the agreement on July 15, 1988, along
with the central bankers of nine other industrialized
nations, setting forth "international . . . regulations
governing the capital adequacy of international banks."[4]

The agreement was signed at the secretive Bank for
International Settlements in Basel, Switzerland, and
was referred to as the Basel Accord. However, since a
second accord was signed in 2004 (which we deal with
in "Behind the Wizard's Curtain"), this agreement is
now referred to as Basel I and the 2004 agreement as
Basel II.

The Bank for International Settlements

I have dealt with the Bank for International Settlements in the two previous articles on the financial crisis

and am going to take the liberty of quoting from them here. First, "A Look Behind the Wizard's Curtain":

Central banks . . . govern a country's monetary policy and create the country's money.

The Bank for International Settlements (BIS), located in Basel, Switzerland, is the central bankers' bank. There are 55 central banks around the planet that are members, but the BIS is controlled by a board of directors, which is comprised of the elite central bankers of 11 different countries (U.S., U.K., Belgium, Canada, France, Germany, Italy, Japan, Switzerland, the Netherlands and Sweden).

Created in 1930, the BIS is owned by its member central banks, which, again, are private entities. The buildings and surroundings that are used for the purpose of the bank are inviolable. No agent of the Swiss public authorities may enter the premises without the express consent of the bank. The bank exercises supervision and police power over its premises. The bank enjoys immunity from criminal and administrative jurisdiction.

In short, they are above the law.
And from the second article, "Hitler's Bank Goes Global":

But then the Bank for International Settlements (BIS) . . . has never seen transparency as one of its core values. In fact, given its fascist pedigree, transparency hasn't been a value at all. Known as Hitler's bank, the Bank for International Settlements worked arm in arm with the Nazis, facilitating the transfer of gold from Nazi-occupied countries to the Reichsbank, and kept their lines open to the international financial community during the Second World War. . . .

It is like a sovereign state. Its personnel have diplomatic immunity for their persons and papers. No taxes are levied on the bank or the personnel's salaries. The grounds are sovereign, as are the buildings and offices. The Swiss government has no legal jurisdiction over the bank and no government agency or authority has oversight over its operations.

Basel I

Basel I established the terms for the minimum capital requirements for the ten central banks that signed the accord: Belgium, Canada, France, Italy, Japan, the Netherlands, the U.K., the U.S., Germany and Sweden (Switzerland signed later).

A standard had been set: banks had to maintain capital of 8 percent of their assets. But according to the agreement, all assets were not the same. Basel I introduced a special system of weighing the risk of different kinds of assets and loans—they referred to it as risk-weighted assets. For example, corporate loans to businesses called for a higher percentage capital than mortgage loans.[5] As a consequence, banks started cutting back on corporate loans and seeking ways to expand their mortgage portfolios.[6]

As for the Japanese banks, they had to adjust. But the Nikkei Index (the Japanese stock market) was booming at the time, so they didn't consider it a big problem. Between 1984 and 1989, the Nikkei had risen from 11,500 to 38,900. As stocks increased in value, the capital base of the Japanese banks (made up largely of stock) increased as well.[7]

Things were cool. Sake flowed, geishas danced, and banker-san was happy. But the good times were short lived. Less than a year later, in May of 1989, the Nikkei began a decline that eventually brought the index down to below eight thousand.[8]

As went the Nikkei, so went the capital structure of the banks. Down they went, slashing their ability to lend and sending the entire Japanese economy into a recession that has been called the "Lost Decade."

You don't cross the Fed and the Bank of England and get away with it. Not on this planet.

It was a different story for the U.S. banks. The new capital adequacy standards laid down as Basel I had loopholes through which the American bankers were able to drive their Porsches to bonuses larger than the budgets of several third-world countries.

The Intentions of Basel I

Writers have referred to the consequences of Basel I as unintended.

Were they really?

Greenspan not only sat on the board of directors of the Bank for International Settlements, he was also of course the chairman of the Federal Reserve Bank. From this position he kept interest rates suppressed at abnormally low levels, ushering in a lethal binge of credit excess in America; advanced the Community Reinvestment Act, which mandated mortgage lending to anyone who drew breath (and some who didn't); and, along with Robert Rubin and Larry Summers, actively fought efforts to regulate the exploding market in toxic financial instruments called derivatives.

This included using his influence to help eliminate laws that had been on the books for decades protecting people from speculative excess and abuse in financial markets (see "The Financial Crisis: A Look Behind the Wizard's Curtain").

Derivatives

Derivatives are what Warren Buffet has called "financial weapons of mass destruction"—financial products that seem to have been imported from a galaxy far, far away.[9]

Derivatives are financial instruments that *derive* their value from some underlying asset. An example of a derivative is one you have heard a lot of lately: mortgage-backed securities.

Here's how this works. Mortgage loans are packaged up and legally pooled into a financial document called a security. This simply means that there is a formal certificate that represents a group of loans. The investor buys the security. The security pays interest to the investor, which is based on the interest rates of the underlying mortgages.

You can see where the name comes from: the financial instrument, the mortgaged-backed security, is *backed* by the mortgages.

It is a derivative because the financial instrument, the security, derives its value from the underlying assets (the mortgage loans).

So what were the intentions of the central bankers when they crafted Basel I? One was to take out the Japanese banks. Mission accomplished.

The other was obvious: to curtail lending to corporations while focusing the attention and appetites of those same lenders on the increased income and bonuses available by investing in mortgage-backed securities.

Under Basel I, banks only had to have half as much capital to invest in mortgages as was required for corporate loans. Or put another way, they could invest twice as much in mortgages as they could in corporate loans with the same amount of capital. The more loans, the more income.

What else did the bankers of Basel think was going to happen other than an explosion in mortgage lending? Nothing of course.

And later, when the lenders bought credit insurance for the securities, the capital requirements were reduced even further, pouring gas on what had by then become a raging inferno of credit speculation.

Credit Default Swaps

It wasn't actually called credit insurance, though. It had another one of those off-planet names, *credit default swaps*, but in essence that's what it was. Here's how this piece of the puzzle fit.

The bank would buy a contract from an insurer that covered the credit risk of the derivative. In other words, the bank would pay a fee to the insurance company—just like an insurance premium—and if the security turned bad, if the loans failed to pay, the insurance company was obligated to cover the bank's loss.[10]

When banks bought credit default swaps for their derivatives from an AAA-rated insurance company, the derivative itself took on an AAA rating.[11]

When the derivative received an AAA rating, the bank's capital requirements—already reduced because the derivatives were made up of mortgages—were reduced even more, freeing up more capital, which enabled them to buy more derivatives, which . . .

There were just a couple of small problems. The credit default swaps—not technically being insurance—were entirely unregulated. This meant that the insurance companies that issued these—think American Insurance Group (AIG), which was the world's largest insurance company and rated AAA, but which is now owned by thee and me—did not have to carry reserves to cover the loss if the trillions of dollars of derivatives they insured went bad.[12]

The other was the fact that with the passage of the Community Reinvestment Act, the mortgage market was awash in subprime loans (borrowers with poor credit, low income, and no or low down payments). And it was these loans that were packaged into mortgage-backed securities by the trillions and sold to virtually every major bank on the planet, making the international financial structure pregnant with disaster.

It was at this point, having originally set the stage, that the world's central bankers returned to the Bank for International Settlements in Basel, Switzerland, and issued a second set of rules referred to as Basel II. Included in the Basel II Accord was an accounting rule called *mark to market*, which brought the planet's entire financial system to its knees (Mark to market is discussed in "Behind the Wizard's Curtain.") Mark to market was like pulling the pin on an enormous hand grenade made up of trillions of dollars of toxic derivatives.

On April 2, 2009, at a meeting of world leaders in London, the final card was played: terrified about the potential consequences of a planetary meltdown, they agreed to a plan that established a global financial dictatorship at the Bank for International Settlements called the Financial Stability Board. And this, dear friends, was the goal from the beginning.

If we are going to be realists, we must acknowledge that Greenspan—along with a few fellow monetary jihadists like Paulson, Rubin, Summers and Geithner—planted the bomb in Basel I, lit the fuse by ensuring any meaningful protection against it was removed, and then detonated it with Basel II. What followed the explosion was a global financial coup, which was executed in April.

It took a while for the fuse to burn and the bomb to detonate, but when viewed as a well-constructed plan, the intentions seem inescapable: this financial crisis was and is a crisis by design.

The story of how Basel II created the worldwide financial crisis and how the Financial Stability Board was created is covered in detail in my earlier articles on this subject: "The Financial Crisis: A Look Behind the Wizard's Curtain" and "Hitler's Bank Goes Global."

It is the second article that spells out what action to take and what can and should be done.

4
The Goldman Connection

August 2009

There will be a war. I'm certain of it.

No, not with Iran, though I'd like to introduce Mahmoud I-refuse-to-wear-a-necktie-under-any-circumstances Ahmadinejad to a woman I met several years ago. She and her twin sister had been experimental subjects of Nazi madman Dr. Josef Mengele. Mengele had tried to change the color of their eyes with dye. The woman was blind. Her sister died at Auschwitz.

Mahmoud, who thinks the Holocaust was a hoax, forgot to pay his brain bill.

And they are a few sandwiches short of a picnic in Pyongyang. Still, I don't think the Chinese will let Kim Jong-il and his newly appointed secret-police-chief son, Kim Jong-un, drag the West into a military confrontation on the Korean peninsula. It's a little too close to home and a Korean War II is not part of Beijing's master plan. At least not yet.

No, this is a war brewing between two iconic American institutions that couldn't be more different: the voice of America's rock culture, *Rolling Stone* magazine, and the country's premier Armani-clad investment bank, Goldman Sachs.

Rolling Stone recently published an article called "The Great American Bubble Machine," a masterful exposé by Matt Taibbi revealing Goldman's greed and corruption in the creation of several investment "bubbles" that have made the firm and its partners—the term *filthy rich* comes to mind—but which have been devastating to Americans and to the U.S. economy.[1]

I rarely use those two words together. I have no problem with people making money—barrels of the stuff. Boat-loads. But this needs to be done with some sense of ethics, some sense of morals, some sense of responsibility toward one's fellow man.

I was informed that Goldman is preparing a response. One wonders if the Wall Street veneer will crack: if they'll come out with their pinstripes pressed and PR guns blazing, trying to marginalize Taibbi.

As those of you who have followed my recent articles on the financial crisis know, I have pointed out the all too coincidental participation of Goldman executives in the creation of the financial crisis. Machiavelli himself would be proud of what has been nothing less than a bloodless takeover of the planet's financial systems. The Guys from Goldman have played their part.

While I have previously drawn attention to a few of the key figures, Taibbi has peeled the onion on several of the investment bank's schemes and has also laid bare the army of Goldman alumni that have turned up at critical decision points in the universe of credit, investment and finance.

His orientation was such that he omitted a few names that I will cover below. But the article is exhaustively researched and ties Goldman to everything from the Great Depression to speculation in oil futures before last year's election that sent gas prices to $5.00 a gallon here in the land of many freeways. My focus, on the other hand, has been exposing the actual cause of the world-wide financial crisis. And our paths have crossed at a few key junctures.

Junctures that bring to mind the great Gordon Gekko— Michael Douglas's character in Oliver Stone's Wall Street. Preening in front of the board of directors and up and down the aisle among the shareholders of Teldar Paper, Douglas shares the philosophy of the successful investment banker as if handing down commandments from Mount Wall Street: "Greed is good. Greed is right. Greed works. Greed clarifies and cuts through and captures the essence of the evolutionary spirit."[2]

Yeah, baby.

But is it more than greed? Are Goldman Sachs' alumni part of a broader agenda that has not only lined their pockets with the spoils of corruption that Taibbi has exposed but has also helped facilitate an international financial coup—a coup that has put the control of the planet's financial affairs into the hands of a small group of central bankers that hold secret meetings at what is nothing less than the Vatican of international finance: the Bank for International Settlements located in Basel, Switzerland?

If you've had a suspicion that bankers are running Washington, then hang on to your Calvins because, while it starts in DC, this story is global in reach and is rolling out before your eyes—if you are willing to look.

Robert Rubin

I could start this part of the story with Henry Fowler, who, after serving as the thirty-fifth Secretary of the Treasury, in 1969 became a partner at Goldman after leaving office. But that's not how things worked in the nineties and beyond. Oh no. The current sequence is very different.

Pictures of Robert Rubin always remind me of the cartoon character Droopy. He seems to be in a perpetual state of sad worry. Hard to know what he's worried about, having received fifty million in compensation from his last employer (Citigroup). Perhaps it's because the financial website *MarketWatch* recently named him as one of the "10 most unethical people in business."[3]

More to the point of our story, having served twenty-six years with Goldman Sachs, ascending to the position of co-chairman, Rubin came to Washington with the Clinton administration as the Assistant to the President for Economic Policy. Bill must have dug the Wall Street touch, because in January of 1995, he appointed Rubin the seventieth United States Secretary of the Treasury.

This could be called the start of what the *New York*

Times has referred to as the modern era of "Government Sachs."[4] The hallmark of Rubin's years in Washington was deregulation—specifically, deregulation of the financial industry. Turn the financial industry loose. Let the big dogs eat. Let them earn. They have Porsche payments to make. Working with Greenspan, he kept interest rates implausibly low and ensured that regulatory safeguards were gunned down like victims in an L.A. drive-by shooting. The Glass-Steagall Act is a prime example. A piece of Depression-era legislation that kept investment banks and commercial banks from committing fiscal incest, it was repealed—charged with being out of touch with the global financial structure.

What it was out of touch with was an agenda to open the floodgates to unbridled speculation by banks that set the industry up for a financial Hiroshima.

It takes a great deal of power and influence to get a federal law repealed in this country—especially one that has served the country well for seventy years. But Rubin, with a little help from his friends—Larry Summers and Alan Greenspan—got it done.

These and other similar actions helped pave the way for an economic crisis that would soon engulf the entire planet.

The housing bubble has burst. The financial services industry is a ward of the state. Insurance companies and automakers are tottering on the brink of bankruptcy. Consumer credit is drying up along with consumer confidence. Banks have stopped lending money, and big corporations have started laying workers off. The stock market is at a five-year low. But amid the greatest financial panic since the Great Depression, the market for one asset stubbornly resists correction: the immaculate reputation of Robert Rubin, former Treasury secretary and pre-eminent economic wise man of the Democratic Party.

. . . But the financial deregulation that allowed markets to boil over began well before President George W. Bush took office. Three decisions relevant to the market meltdown . . . can be attributed to Rubin."

—Timothy Noah[5]

Mexico

Let's set aside for the moment that when Rubin was co-chairman of Goldman, the firm underwrote billions of dollars in bonds for the Mexican government. When the Mexican peso tanked a few years later, Rubin, as Secretary of the Treasury, arranged a multibillion-dollar taxpayer bailout, which, according to reports, saved Goldman a cool $4 billion. Kind of a dress rehearsal for Hank Paulson's trillion-dollar raid on the U.S. Treasury, which channeled tens of billions into the womb from which he came—Mother Goldman. But we'll get to that.

Rubin did more than pave the road to a financial Armageddon with Maestro Greenspan. His spawn have helped ensure that the crisis came off as planned and that it was solved with the creation of a global financial dictator, who—prepare to be shocked—is also a Goldman alum. But, again, I'm getting ahead of myself.

The Acolytes

Summers

At Treasury, Rubin groomed two protégés that helped craft the multitrillion-dollar financial bailout and that are today in charge of U.S. financial policy: Larry Summers and Timothy Geithner.

Summers, though not a formal Goldman alum, is a fully certified Rubin deregulation clone. He was *chief economist for the World Bank* in the early '90s and later served as Rubin's Deputy Secretary of the Treasury. When Rubin left, Summers took full control of Treasury for the last year and a half of the Clinton administration. Today Summers is the director of the National Economic Council, which means he is in the commanding position of being the senior advisor to President Obama on domestic and international economic policy.

Geithner

Timothy Geithner, like Summers, worked for Rubin at Treasury during the Clinton administration and was a Rubin favorite. He stayed on during Summers' tenure and then snagged the powerful presidency of the New York Federal Reserve Bank. It was Rubin who got Geithner the gig at the New York Fed and it was Rubin who hooked him up with Obama, who appointed him as his Secretary of the Treasury.

In case there is any doubt about Geithner's loyalties, it is widely known on Wall Street and inside the Beltway, that Goldman filed adoption papers on him years ago.

> In an interview on July 3, 2009, the former US Assistant Secretary of the Treasury, Paul Craig Roberts, was asked "Does the US Secretary of the Treasury work for the people or does he work for the banking system on Wall Street?" to which he replied, "Geithner works for Goldman Sachs."[6]

So, for those who thought that Rubin had left the stage of U.S. economic policy, think again. Because not only has Rubin himself been named as an advisor to President Obama, but another of his groupies, Christina Romer, has been named as the chair of the White House Council of Economic Advisors.

Even today, then, Goldman's former co-chairman is advising Obama behind the scenes and his acolytes are in charge of the U.S. Treasury (Geithner) and the White House Council of Economic Advisors (Romer) and the National Economic Council (Summers). The White House Council of Economic Advisors is made up of academicians who provide the President with economic statistics and other information on domestic and international financial matters. The National Economic Council brings together key administration players and agency heads to coordinate and see to the implementation of the administration's economic policy. The director (Summers) is the President's senior economic advisor.

You'd think with this crew in place, Goldman would have had the White House covered. But Obama apparently went for their two-for-one sale. In addition to Rubin, another former Goldman chairman, the controversial Jon Corzine, has been a top Obama economic advisor. In fact he was on the short list to become Secretary of the Treasury. But Rubin ruled and Geithner got the gig.

Given that Goldman employees gave more money to Obama ($994,000) than any other commercial enterprise in the United States, and that the White House is awash in Goldmanites, it is no surprise that 1600 Pennsylvania Avenue is viewed as one of the bank's more important operating divisions.[7]

Patterson

Even with the White House under control, Geithner beefed up his G-man staff at Treasury. He named yet another Goldmanite as his chief of staff. Mark Patterson was selected to help him run the government's financial circus. Patterson gave up his plum position as the Vice President for Government Relations at Goldman—meaning he was the investment bank's chief lobbyist—to become the number two man at Treasury.

I know, I know. Obama said no lobbyists in his administration; but, well, Mark is family. Sort of a fiscal fraternity brother—Alpha Delta Goldman.

Henry Paulson

But before Obama was Bush. And with oh-so-propitious timing, before the news of the financial crisis began to go mainline in 2007, a new Goldman CEO descended from his throne on Wall Street to come to Washington and help his government manage the nation's financial affairs.

We love you, Hank.

Viewed from the board rooms of Wall Street, Henry Paulson's blitzkrieg of the nation's capital was nothing short of stunning: a George Patton in pinstripes—except Patton was fighting a real enemy, not one that he himself had created.

Liar, Liar, Pants on Fire

At first, he used PR spin to calm the multitudes. As the crisis began to unravel in August 2007, Paulson assured the American people that the subprime mortgage problems were nothing to be concerned about, that they would remain contained due to the strong global economy.

> Reuters: U.S. Treasury Secretary Henry Paulson said on Wednesday that the market impact of the U.S. subprime mortgage fallout is largely contained and that the global economy is as strong as it has been in decades.[8]

Not.

The stock market peaked two months later followed by a crash that wiped out trillions.

In July of 2008, after the fall of IndyMac Bank, Paulson told the public that the banking system was safe and sound and that the situation was very "manageable." Twenty-five banks failed in 2008. Sixty-four have gone under in the first six and a half months of 2009. Another 309 are now listed as "problem banks."[10]

In fact, according to FDIC chairman, Sheila Bair, in March 2009, unless the FDIC gets more revenue, they themselves are going to be broke.

"Without additional revenue beyond the regular assessments, current projections indicate that the fund balance will approach zero."[11]

In a television interview on *Meet the Press* on August 10, 2008, Paulson stated that he would not be putting any capital into Fannie Mae or Freddie Mac.* Three weeks later, he took them over and committed $200 billion in bailout funds; $60 billion has already been spent.[12]

When I was growing up, we'd call this kind of guy a "bullshit artist." But that didn't stop him from staging a raid on the U.S. Treasury in broad daylight that would have made Dillinger drool with envy. This, while Congress—a Democratic Congress at that—stood around with their thumbs up their butts.

Ed Liddy

AIG.

Perhaps nothing quite so demonstrated this scam as the government bailout of American International Group

---

*Fannie Mae, Freddie Mac—Federal National Mortgage Association, Federal Home Loan Mortgage Corporation. Fannie was established in 1938 to turn mortgages into securities to be sold to investors. Fannie dealt in the primary home loan market. Freddie was established in 1970 to compete with Freddie to facilitate the secondary mortgage market. They were Government Sponsored Enterprises (GSE's); now they are in receivership held by the US government.

(AIG), the country's largest insurance company. On September 16, 2008, Paulson coughed up $85 billion of your tax dollars to take control of AIG. The $85 billion loan got the government 80 percent ownership of the insurance giant. Just what I always wanted from my government, a bankrupt insurance company.[13]

It turns out the $85 billion wasn't enough. AIG has continued to hemorrhage losses and Uncle has now poured a total of $182 billion into the insurance company.

Jefferson and Adams weep.

Sticky constitutional issues aside, many have found it more than curious that when the government granted the loan, AIG turned right around and paid it out to the investment banks to which it owed money. The bank that got the largest payout was . . . of course, Goldman Sachs—a cool $13 billion.[14] The money simply passed from your paycheck to the U.S. Treasury, from the Treasury to AIG and from AIG to Goldman (and other banks).

Naturally, Paulson didn't provide the loan without ensuring that Goldman and fellow banksters would be repaid in full. No, no. He made sure the transfers would occur without any objection from AIG or unseemly negotiations with the banks.[15] To do this, he tapped Goldman Sachs board member, Ed Liddy, to be the new CEO of AIG.

The good-hearted Mr. Liddy took the gig for a dollar a year in salary from AIG. But he held on to his $3 million in Goldman stock.

Cute, eh?

Goldman made billions from AIG earlier as well. AIG didn't know this. Neither did Goldman's clients. You see, despite the fact that they had collected enormous fees selling financial products that were "insured" by AIG, Goldman simultaneously sold AIG short. You get this? On the one hand, they sold financial instruments to their clients, which carried high investment ratings because AIG insured the buyer against loss. At the same time, they made investment "bets" for their own account against AIG. Estimates are that they made $4.7 billion betting against AIG while selling the AIG-guaranteed products to their clients.

> "Greed clarifies and cuts through and captures the essence of the evolutionary spirit."
>
> —Gordon Gekko

AIG behind him, Hammering Hank marched on.

Lehman Brothers

Paulson had worked out strategies to have Bear Stearns purchased by J.P. Morgan in March of '08 and had committed $200 billion to rescue Freddie and Fannie in early September, but when Goldman's chief rival, Lehman Brothers, began to waver in midsummer, he turned a blind eye. Lehman went bankrupt and sent the already declining stock market into a colossal rout. The next day, he helped arrange an $85 billion bailout for AIG.

Following Lehman's collapse, Goldman and Morgan Stanley were the only remaining pure investment banks left on Wall Street.

The Bailout

Congress was next.

Attila the Hun had nothing on Paulson and his lap dog, Ben Bernanke, and their assault on Congress, with threats of riots and martial law as they fear-mongered the Troubled Asset Relief Program (TARP) through the House and Senate—winding up with a cool trillion dollars to "save" the banks.[16]

Congress's actions remind me of a bad Godzilla movie, with masses of panicked Japanese citizens fleeing the fire-breathing monster, which is lumbering through the city toppling buildings and devouring cars.

The legislation drafted by our elected officials sounds like something issued to Stalin by the Politburo. They granted Paulson complete dictatorial powers over the bailout money. The TARP read in part:

Decisions by the Secretary pursuant to the authority of this Act are non-reviewable and committed to agency discretion, and may not be reviewed by any court of law or any administrative agency.[17]

Calling the multibillion-dollar bailout a "stimulus"

program is but a cruel joke. This was nothing more complicated than another burglary in plain daylight—a theft of hundreds of billions of dollars from American taxpayers into the Armani-clad arms of major Wall Street banks.

You won't be surprised to learn, I'm sure, that Goldman Sachs got a cool $10 billion of TARP funds. And if you followed the billions pouring from your paychecks to Wall Street, you might remember that Bank of America at first received $25 billion. Then, in the midst of the chaos, they agreed to purchase Merrill Lynch. As it turned out, however, Merrill's losses were $15 billion more than B of A had expected. This was due in part to $4 billion in bonuses paid out by Merrill's CEO, John Thain, who pushed the bonuses through his books just before the Bank of America deal closed.[18]

Bank of America was taken by surprise by the losses and the purchase of Merrill Lynch started to go shaky, to which Comrade Paulson coughed up another $20 billion of your tax dollars.[19]

You guys are so cool bailing out these banks. I mean it. It brings tears to my eyes.

Oh, I should mention that John Thain, the guy who pushed through the last-minute billions in bonuses, had been the president and co-chief operating officer at Goldman Sachs before becoming the president of Merrill Lynch.

Robert K. Steel: Treasury to Wachovia

Another Goldman alum to drive his bank headlong into the merger-mania chaos of the financial crisis was Robert Steel. Steel had worked with Paulson at Goldman for thirty years and eventually rose to the position of vice chairman of the firm.

He followed Paulson to the U.S. Treasury in 2006 and became his top financial policy advisor. In July of 2008, he left the government and became the CEO of Wachovia bank, the sixth largest bank in the country.

How did he wind up at Wachovia? Three weeks earlier, Wachovia—who had paid Goldman Sachs $77 million in fees for financial advice—also sought their assistance in finding a new CEO.[20]

Steel was the man. Three short months later, Steel struck a deal with Citibank to buy Wachovia—a deal that required hundreds of billions in loan guarantees from the government. Then he changed his mind and sold Wachovia to Wells Fargo without the government involved and became a member of the Wells Fargo board of directors.

According to Taibbi's article:

. . . Robert Steel, the former Goldmanite head of Wachovia, scored himself and his fellow executives $225 million in golden-parachute payments as his bank was self-destructing.[21]

Other articles claim that Steel himself did not take a bonus.

Regardless, you have Goldman getting millions in fees to advise Wachovia on, among other things, the selection of a new CEO, who, it turns out, is a former *Goldman vice chairman*. Nothing illegal about it, but the financial incest begins to smell pornographic.

Neel Kashkari: TARP Front Man

Paulson is nothing if not thorough. While he ultimately called the shots, he brought in someone else to oversee the allocation of the TARP funds and take the congressional heat. This was thirty-five-year-old *Goldman vice president*, Neel Kashkari, who, as the head of the Office of Financial Stability at Treasury, was in control of the $700 billion in bailout funds. It was Kashkari who had to testify about the TARP to Congress—a hot seat whose temperature started to soar shortly after Paulson's scam began to dawn on the legislators.

The Takeover

There were others. In fact, Paulson brought so many former Goldman executives to Treasury the *New York Times* noted the "appearance that the Treasury Department has become a de facto Goldman division."

These included:

Reuben Jeffrey, a *former managing partner of Goldman's European Financial Institutions Group* in London;

Dan Jester, a former *Goldman vice president*;

Steve Shafran, *long-time Paulson associate at Goldman*;

Kendrick Wilson III, a *managing partner at Goldman in the Financial Institutions Group*; and

Edward Forst, a *former executive vice president and chief administrative officer at Goldman.*

Current or veteran Goldman executives all, they worked on everything from the bailout of Fannie and Freddie to the capital restructuring of the nation's banks.

All of which makes Andy Borowitz's satirical article in the July 16, 2009, *Huffington Post* that much more understandable. The lead reads:

In what some on Wall Street are calling the biggest blockbuster deal in the history of the financial sector, Goldman Sachs confirmed today that it was in talks to acquire the U.S. Department of the Treasury.[22]

No surprise that the first two people I showed the article to thought it was real.

The White House: Joshua Bolten

Paulson and his Goldman gladiators also had air cover from the White House. George Bush's Chief of Staff during the bailout blizzard was none other than Josh Bolten. Bolten had become Chief of Staff in April of 2006 and is credited with persuading the President to recruit Paulson as the Treasury Secretary.

No surprise, since Bolten had been the *executive director, Legal & Government Affairs for Goldman Sachs International* before joining the Bush 2000 presidential campaign.

Powerful friends. Powerful places.

But the Goldman virus has not been confined to the White House and the Treasury, not by a long shot.

The Derivatives Boom

Neil Levin

The acknowledged bogeymen of the world's financial crisis were mortgages, many of which were subprime, packaged up into investment products called mortgage-backed securities—also called derivatives because the package, the security, *derived* its value from the underlying mortgages. There is much more to this story (see "The Financial Crisis: A Look Behind the Wizard's Curtain"), but the point here is that these mortgages were a critical component to the crisis.

For reasons we detailed in a follow-up article, "The Financial Crisis: The Hidden Beginning", the explosive growth of these products was due in large part to the fact that the securities carried an AAA investment-grade rating. That rating was granted because Goldman Sachs and other banks were able to purchase what was essentially credit insurance for the investment. In other words, if the investment went bad, it was "insured" against loss.

This kind of protection was called a *credit default swap*. Though "swaps" looked like insurance and acted like insurance, they were remarkably adjudicated not to be so, thus eliminating the need for the "insurer" to hold reserves against possible losses. This opened the door to a torrent of speculation in the derivatives.

Let Matt Taibbi tell it.

AIG, a major purveyor of default swaps, approached the New York State Insurance Department in 2000 and asked whether default swaps would be regulated as insurance. At the time, the office was run by one Neil Levin, a *former Goldman vice president*, who decided against regulating the swaps. Now freed to underwrite as many housing-based securities and buy as much credit-default protection as it wanted, Goldman went berserk with lending lust. By the peak of the housing boom in 2006, Goldman was underwriting $76.5 billion worth of mortgage-backed securities—a third of which were subprime—much of it to institutional investors like pensions and insurance companies.[23] (italics mine)

The Commodities Exchange

Gary Gensler

But not to worry. We're protected now. The regulation of many derivatives and other exotic financial instruments—the $5 trillion commodity futures industry (gold, silver, oil, treasury bills, corn, cotton, sugar, etc.)—has recently been delegated by President Obama to Gary Gensler.

Gensler was confirmed as the head of the Commodity Futures Trading Commission (CFTC) in May, but it took a little arm twisting. Some members of Congress had misgivings.

You see back in 2000, when he was at Treasury, Gensler advocated legislation—which eventually passed— exempting credit default swaps and some other derivatives from regulation.

Still, it's hard to argue with his understanding of derivatives. He spent eighteen years at Goldman Sachs, the most aggressive derivative trader on Wall Street, where he became a *partner*. He subsequently went to the Treasury Department where he pushed for the deregulation of the industry. Now President Obama has put him in charge of it.

Change we can believe in . . .

The New York Stock Exchange

Duncan Niederauer

Goldman alumni control not only the commodities markets but the major stock markets of the world as well. In May of 2007, the granddaddy of stock markets, the New York Stock Exchange (NYSE), bought Euronext (a pan-European stock exchange with subsidiaries in Belgium, France, Netherlands, Portugal, and the United Kingdom), which, now branded as NYSE Euronext, operates the largest securities exchange on the planet.

To run the show, the newly combined entity brought in Duncan Niederauer and appointed him chief executive officer. Niederauer had been a *partner and managing director at Goldman Sachs* before joining NYSE Euronext.

The New York Fed

Stephen Friedman

The Federal Reserve System controls the country's money supply. Nice gig if you can get it. It is made up of a Board of Governors (seven), appointed by the President for fourteen-year terms. There are twelve Federal Reserve Banks around the country. The New York Fed is a first among equals. An institution of awesome power, it supervises and controls the major money center banks in New York, the capital of the U.S. financial industry.

The New York Fed worked closely with Treasury Secretary Paulson on numerous aspects of the bailout during the chaos of the financial meltdown in the fall and winter of '08.

Much of this work was carried out by Timothy Geithner, then president of the New York Fed, until Rubin helped get him the job as the Secretary of the Treasury. The chairman of the New York Fed at this time was Stephen Friedman. He picked up the reins when Geithner left while looking for a replacement.

Friedman was a former *CEO of Goldman Sachs* and later chairman at Goldman. He'd left Goldman in 2002 to oversee economic policy in the Bush White House as the chairman of the National Economic Council. Later, Bush appointed him to the chairmanship of the President's Foreign Intelligence Advisory Board.

In 2004, he returned to New York and the

chairmanship of the Fed. In addition, he returned to Goldman to become its chairman while he was also the chairman of the Federal Reserve Bank of New York.

William Dudley

To replace Geithner as president of the NY Fed, Friedman selected William Dudley. Dudley had been a *partner and managing director at Goldman Sachs* for ten years prior to the Fed appointment.

Incest doesn't begin to say it.

From the White House to Treasury, from the New York Fed to AIG, from the Commodity Futures Trading Commission to the New York Stock Exchange, Goldman is there.

The World Bank and the International Monetary Fund

Robert Zoellick

But it doesn't stop at our shores. It's a global economy today, which requires global control.

The World Bank was founded in 1945 to help with the reconstruction of Europe after the Second World War. Over the years, their mission changed.

Today they claim that their purpose is to eliminate world poverty—kind of a pinstriped Mother Theresa for the planet.[24] Unfortunately, this is at odds with what they actually do. If they were achieving their aims, the countries that they worked with would be prospering. But the reverse is true. In fact, an objective view of the results of the bank's activities leads one to the inescapable conclusion that what the World Bank produces is indebted nations.[25]

In their beneficence, the World Bank makes loans to third-world countries, countries that can't borrow elsewhere. The loans carry conditions that dictate domestic policy "adjustments" in health, education, tax policy, judicial matters, agriculture, manufacturing . . .

You get the picture. The bank and its sister organization, the International Monetary Fund, have about three-quarters of the planet in debt like this. Sarah Anderson, the Director of The Global Economy Program of the Institute for Policy Studies in Washington put an interesting spin on it:

> Medieval doctors always prescribed the same "cure"; no matter what the ailment, they applied leeches to patients and bled them. For the past decade and a half, critics have likened the World Bank and the International Monetary Fund (IMF) to these doctors. The two institutions have thrown millions of people deeper into poverty by promoting the same harsh economic reforms . . . regardless of local culture, resources or economic context. Strapped with heavy debts, most developing countries have reluctantly accepted these

reforms, known as structural adjustment programs (SAPS), as a condition for receiving IMF
or World Bank loans.

In recent years, the doctors' harsh medicine
has been exposed in dozens of studies and in
increasingly vocal street protests. In response, the
World Bank and the IMF have been attempting
to revamp their public image into that of anti-
poverty crusaders.[26]

The president of the World Bank is Robert Zoellick. In this position, Zoellick walks in the shoes of
great humanitarians like über-neocon, Paul Wolfowitz,
"architect of the Iraq War," and Robert McNamara, the
Johnny Appleseed of Agent Orange.

Zoellick is in charge of spreading loans around the
world to eliminate poverty, not unlike McNamara's
blanketing of Southeast Asia with Agent Orange to
stop Communism. Both agendas produce the same
results—toxicity and, in some cases, death—of the cor-
poral body or the body politic.

Prior to joining the World Bank, Zoellick served as
vice chairman, international, of the Goldman Sachs Group.

You gotta love these guys.

The World Bank and the International Monetary
Fund (whose current most powerful board member is
our very own Timothy Geithner) are the key tacticians
in ensuring that the planet's smaller economies remain
deeply in debt. But they are no longer at the apex of
international finance today.

As I have made clear in our earlier articles, the purpose of this financial crisis was to take down the United States and the U.S. dollar as the stable datum of planetary finance and, in the midst of the resulting confusion, put in its place a Global Monetary Authority—a planetary financial control organization to "ensure this never happens again."

This purpose has now been accomplished.

To explain how, I quote from an article I wrote on this subject a few months ago ("Hitler's Bank Goes Global").

The Financial Stability Board

On April 2, 2009, the members of the G-20 (a loose-knit organization of the central bankers and finance ministers of the 20 major industrialized nations) issued a communiqué that gave birth to what is no less than Big Brother in a three-piece suit.

The communiqué announced the creation of the all too Soviet sounding Financial Stability Board (FSB). *The Financial Stability Board.* Remember that name well, because they now have control of the planet's finances . . . and, when one peels the onion of the communiqué, control of much, much more.

The Twelve International Standards and Codes

While several press releases from the G-20's London conclave reference these codes as though they were handed down from a fiscal Mount Sinai, finding the specifics takes some digging.

But then the Bank for International Settlements (BIS)—out of which the FSB operates—has never seen transparency as one of its core values. In fact, given its fascist pedigree, transparency hasn't been a value at all.

Known as Hitler's bank, the Bank for International Settlements worked arm in arm with the Nazis, facilitating the transfer of gold from Nazi-occupied countries to the Reichsbank, and kept their lines open to the international financial community during the Second World War.

The BIS is completely above the law.

It is like a sovereign state. Its personnel have diplomatic immunity for their persons and papers. No taxes are levied on the bank or the personnel's salaries. The grounds are sovereign, as are the buildings and offices. The Swiss government has no legal jurisdiction over the bank and no government agency or authority has oversight over its operations.

In a 2003 article titled "Controlling the World's Monetary System: The Bank for International Settlements," Joan Veon wrote:

> The BIS is where all of the world's central banks meet to analyze the global economy and determine what course of action they will take next to put more money in their pockets, since they control the amount of money in circulation and how much interest they are going to charge governments and banks for borrowing from them...

When you understand that the BIS pulls the strings of the world's monetary system, you then understand that they have the ability to create a financial boom or bust in a country. If that country is not doing what the money lenders want, then all they have to do is sell its currency.

And if you don't find that troubling, the Key International Standards and Codes just adopted by the Financial Stability Board cover such things as:

- specification of the structure and functions of government;(!)

- data gathering from ministries of education, health, finance and other agencies;

- matters dealing with personal savings accounts and retirement incomes.

Here's an example of the FSB in action, from an article written by former Clinton advisor and political strategist Dick Morris for *The Bulletin* on April 6, 2009.

The FSB is also charged with "implementing… tough new principles on pay and compensation and to support sustainable compensation schemes and the corporate social responsibility of all firms."

That means that the FSB will regulate how much executives are to be paid and will enforce its idea of corporate social responsibility at "all firms."

Almost no one on the planet has grasped what has occurred here.

Most central banks are answerable to no one. The U.S. Federal Reserve, for instance, is a private bank. It is owned by shareholders. Yes, the President appoints the chairman, and the chairman must testify before Congress, but no one gives them orders or tells them what to do. Again, they are a private, not government, institution (a very good reason to support Ron Paul's bill [H.R. 1207] calling for congressional authority to audit the Fed—something they currently have no right to do).

And it is the newly created Financial Stability Board, operating as an arm of the Bank for International Settlements, that *now structures and dictates the rules and regulations* to be carried out by the central banks of the world. And given the fact that central banks essentially operate independently of their national congresses or parliaments, the FSB *now controls the monetary policy of the planet.*

It is now, for all practical purposes, the Politburo of international finance. And who is the chairman of this little known entity based in Basel, Switzerland? Mario Draghi. Draghi was *a partner at Goldman Sachs* until, like Henry Paulson, he left Goldman in 2006. Paulson took over the U.S. Treasury and Draghi became the governor of the Bank of Italy (Italy's central bank) and in April of this year, chairman of the Financial Stability Board.

Goldman Alum's Control

Draghi is also a member of the board of directors of the Bank for International Settlements. In fact, the BIS board reads like a Goldman reunion committee:

Mark Carney had a thirteen-year career with Goldman Sachs, where he became the *managing director of Investment Banking* before becoming the governor of the Bank of Canada and a member of the BIS board.

William Dudley, president of the New York Fed and *former partner at Goldman Sachs*, is also a member of the board, along with Draghi.

And there you have it. *Goldman alumni* in complete financial control of U.S. financial policy and markets, from the White House and Treasury to the New York Fed, the New York Stock Exchange and the Commodity Futures Trading Commission. At the international level, they were in positions of power at the World Bank, the International Monetary Fund, the Bank for International Settlements, and its newly created fiscal overlord, the Financial Stability Board.

This is my fourth article in a series about the financial crisis. Despite our exposure of what some commentators have called Goldman's economic terrorism, it is important to understand that they are but a part—soldiers in pinstripes—of a more basic agenda, which is nearly complete at this point.

This agenda is set forth in my previous articles—"A Look Behind the Wizard's Curtain", "Hitler's Bank Goes Global and The Hidden Beginning".

But "nearly complete" is not a *fait accompli*. And so I refer you again to articles one and two, the closing paragraphs of both set out specific actions to take to help bring this situation under control.

Goldman is like a Rottweiler on a leash. The key is bringing the handler, the Bank for International Settlements, under control.

5
Preparing for the Money Meltdown

October 2009

I wrote my senator about the bailout.

The little one: Paulson and Bernanke's $700 billion donation to their favorite charity, Wall Street.

I urged her to rethink a commitment of nearly three-quarters of a trillion dollars of taxpayer money—my money and yours—when we had no way to pay it back other than going cap in hand to our friends in the Chinese Communist Party and Dubai to try to borrow it.

I say *try*, because for years Congress has been spending hundreds of billions of dollars a year more than it takes in and our Marxist and Muslim bankers are getting more than a little skeptical about whether we will ever be able to repay them.

No wonder. We are currently in debt more than $11 trillion, and this is just the government IOUs like Treasury bills and Treasury bonds.[1] Forget the money Congress has ripped off from the Social Security program and the tens of trillions more of unfunded liabilities (future financial commitments for which we do not have the money; estimates run to about $99 trillion).[2]

These numbers are so big they break the mind. It's hard to even fathom what they mean:

If you laid one-dollar bills end to end, you could make a chain that stretches from Earth to the moon and back again two hundred times before you ran out of dollar bills! It would take a military jet flying at the speed of sound, reeling out a roll of dollar bills behind it, fourteen years before it reeled out one trillion dollar bills.[3]

You get the picture.

The interest on the national debt last year was $451,000,000,000. That's $1,235,616,438 a day, $51,484,018 an hour, $858,066 a minute, $14,301 a second.[4]

Makes you feel warm all over, doesn't it? So I told my senator to knock it off.

She responded. She said that eighty-eight people had written in opposing the bail out and that five thousand had written in, in favor of it. But that this was a national crisis and she and the other members of Congress felt they were doing the right thing for the American people.

Arrogance doesn't even begin to say it.

These legislators, who have the financial IQ of roadkill, who have bankrupted our nation to the point of half a trillion dollars a year in interest for wars and welfare, know what's best for the American people?

The first bailout, which was a catastrophe, is of course, now being followed with a second that has more pork than a Jimmy Dean sausage factory.* This one is now branded as a "stimulus package" and is being muscled through Congress as I write this for a cool trillion and a quarter (including interest).[5]

You'd think someone had pumped LSD into the drinking water up there. With the new bailout-program-cum-stimulus-plan, the projected budget deficit for this year alone is about $1.8 trillion.

Where do they think they are going to get this money? Foreign central banks are dumping dollars like a bad habit, and U.S. debt is now about as welcome as an envelope of anthrax.

Which brings us to the point of this article, which is that when the government finishes their spending binge, and wakes up to their eye-watering fiscal hangover, they will turn inward with a vengeance, seeking to filch money from every nook and cranny of the U.S. population.

Tax Increases on the Wealthy

That there will be tax increases is a given. And they will start with the affluent. If you have worked hard and accumulated some wealth in the process, you are a high-profile target for higher taxes.

---

*Pork—short for pork barrel politics. Where a national politician arm twists his fellows to get part of the national budget allocated to a pet project back home. For example, a local airport named in honor of the politician built at the cost of millions but which serves ten flights per day, mostly to and from Washington.

There is strong sentiment from the White House on down that if you make decent money, if you have accumulated some assets, the government should take part of it and spread it around.

Everyone is familiar with the President's statement to Joe the Plumber during a campaign stop last October when he said, "I think when you spread the wealth around, it's good for *everybody*"—everybody being those people who didn't earn the money but who get some of yours.

But let's not quibble about who created the wealth; what's important is to spread it around, even things out.

And in case you're not mainlining MSNBC for your political news these days, you might have missed the fact that this point of view is not the sole province of the White House.

Some key members of Congress are very clear about their Das Kapitalian intentions.*

Barney Frank, the chairman of the House Financial Services Committee, noted recently:

> "I think at this point there needs to be a focus on an immediate increase in spending and I think this is a time when deficit fear has to take a second seat. . . . I believe later on there should be tax increases. Speaking personally, I think there are a

---

*Das Kapitalian—Das Kapital (1867) by Karl Marx, one of the founders of communism. Developed the idea of political economy as a point of social justice leading to the distribution of wealth.

lot of very rich people out there whom we can tax at a point down the road."

In fact, the good congressman may seek a shortcut to your income. Instead of waiting for your tax return, your salary itself could be at risk.

An article in *Financial Week* quotes the chairman of the powerful Financial Services Committee as saying:

> Congress will consider legislation to extend some of the curbs on executive pay that now apply only to those banks receiving federal assistance. . . . The compensation restrictions would apply to all financial institutions and *might be extended to include all U.S. companies.*[6] [Emphasis added]

Channeling Karl Marx, Democratic Representative James Moran, Frank's colleague in the House, had this to say during a campaign stop:

> In the last several years, we have had the highest corporate profit ever in American history... but it hasn't been shared. And that's the problem. Because we have been guided by a Republican administration who believes in the simplistic notion that people who have wealth are entitled to keep it. And they have an antipathy toward the means of redistributing wealth.

Say what?

See, here's the scary part: he's serious. He is a United States congressman on the Appropriations Committee—one of the most important and powerful committees in the House. He is also part of the Democratic leadership in the House, and this man thinks there is something wrong with people who consider that when they have accumulated some assets they are entitled to keep them.

When you add gargantuan budget deficits to a government whose economic philosophy is grounded in a craving to redistribute the wealth of its citizens, you know they will be coming for those that have managed to flourish and prosper.

Let's be blunt: if you earn well or you have assets, your financial statement is at risk.

But the assault on your assets is not just coming from potential changes in tax policy.

Confiscation of Personal Retirement Accounts

Testimony before the House Committee on Education a few months ago suggested that personal retirement accounts (IRAs and 401Ks) should be converted into government-controlled accounts called Guaranteed Retirement Accounts (GRAs).[8] They would be managed by that bastion of fiscal propriety the Social Security Administration.

California Democrat George Miller's House Committee on Education and Labor heard a proposal from
Teresa Ghilarducci, director of the Schwartz Center for Economic Policy Analysis at the New School
for Social Research in New York, to eliminate tax
breaks for 401(k) and similar retirement accounts
such as IRAs and convert them into Guaranteed
Retirement Accounts managed by the Social Security
Administration.[9]

The Plan

Under Ghilarducci's plan, employees would have 5
percent of their pay mandatorily deducted from their
pay and deposited into their GRA. This deduction
would be in addition to Social Security and Medicare
taxes, which would also have to continue being paid by
employers.

The 5 percent would not be deductible by employers (as Social Security and Medicare taxes are), and
only half of the GRA assets could be passed along to
your heirs at death. Presumably, Uncle would keep the
other half.

"I'm just rearranging the breaks that are available
now for 401(k)s and spreading the wealth," she said.[10]

There's that phrase again.

Argentina to Confiscate Retirement Plans

And just in case you think the idea of a government confiscating personal retirement accounts is out of the range of possibility, we urge you to read the story in the October 22, 2008, issue of the *Wall Street Journal*, which reported that the Argentinean government had seized all private pension and retirement accounts to fund government operations and a ballooning budget deficit.

Some articles note that this program was mandated by the President but still had to be approved by the Argentinean Congress, which is controlled by the President's Peronist political party.[11]

In reporting this possibility, I walk a tight line of trying not to be alarmist, yet not shying away from communicating the information that people should have about their savings, reserves and investments.

In that regard, it is important to understand that there is no current legislation pending on this matter, and besides Ghilarducci's testimony, I have heard nothing formal that I can substantiate which would validate that such a plan is imminent.

Still, the article dated October 21, 2008, by the widely respected Ambrose Evans-Pritchard, who writes for the *UK Telegraph*, is of interest:

Argentina seizes pension funds to pay debts. Who's next?
Here is a warning to us all. The Argentine state

is taking control of the country's privately-managed pension funds in a drastic move to raise cash.

Should we worry about our pensions?

It is a foretaste of what may happen across the world as governments discover that tax revenue, and discover that the bond markets are unwilling to plug the gap. The G7* states are already acquiring an unhealthy taste for the arbitrary seizure of private property, I notice. . . .

So, over $29 billion of Argentine civic savings are to be used as a funding kitty for the populist antics of President Cristina Kirchner. This has been dressed up as an anti-corruption and efficiency move. Aren't they always? . . .

The funds being targeted are known as AFJPs or retirement accounts, but how long will it now be before Mrs. Kirchner cracks down on the entire $97 billion pool of private pensions? There are a lot of much-needed hard currency assets in those portfolios. . . .

President Kirchner has been eyeing the pension pool for some time. Last year she pushed through

---

*G7—A group of finance ministers from the seven largest industrialized nations. No developing nations are allowed.

new rules forcing them to invest more money inside the country—always a warning signal.

My fear is that governments in the US, Britain, and Europe will display similar reflexes. Indeed, they have already done so. The forced-feeding of banks with fresh capital—whether they want it or not—and the seizure of the Fannie/Freddie mortgage giants before they were in fact in trouble (in order to prevent a Chinese buying strike of US bonds and prevent a spike in US mortgage rates), shows that private property can be co-opted—or eliminated—with little due process if that is required to serve the collective welfare. This is a slippery slope. (emphasis mine)[12]

Confiscation of Gold and Silver

But trillion-dollar budget deficits will require more.

Many turn to precious metals during times of economic duress. This is no surprise, as gold and silver have been a store of value for thousands of years and they have actual productive uses as opposed to paper currency, which has none other than its government-mandated use as money.

When a government has debased its currency at the printing press, it often takes measures to try to prevent its citizens from fleeing from the currency into precious metals or stronger currencies. One of the measures that has been used in the past is making the ownership of precious metals illegal. This seeks to stop the capital flight from its currency to hard assets.

Sound unreal?

We give you President Franklin D. Roosevelt on March 9, 1933:

> . . . I, as President, do declare that . . . the continued private hoarding of gold and silver by subjects of the United States poses a grave threat to the peace, equal justice, and well-being of the United States; and that appropriate measures must be taken immediately to protect the interests of our people.

> Therefore. . . I hereby proclaim that such gold and silver holdings are prohibited, and that all such coin, bullion or other possessions of gold and silver be tendered within fourteen days to agents of the Government of the United States for compensation at the official price. . . .

> All safe deposit boxes in banks or financial institutions have been sealed. . . .

> Therefore be advised that your vault box must remain sealed, and may only be opened in the presence of an agent of the Internal Revenue Service.[13]

It may surprise you to know that laws still exist that give the President the authority to prohibit the ownership of gold, silver and other assets during emergencies. The Trading with the Enemy Act and the International Emergency Economic Powers Act can be used to freeze privately held assets and prohibit their possession anytime the President issues a proclamation of emergency.

Currency Controls

Currency controls are yet another way governments try to contain the adverse effects of printing too much money.

Wikipedia defines it this way: "Currency control is a system whereby a country tries to regulate the value of money (currency) within its borders."[14]

This can take many forms, but for our purposes, one of the ways governments implement currency controls is to limit or prevent assets from leaving the country. You might not be able to move money or other assets abroad (as that would take them out of the grasp of Uncle). Converting dollars into a stronger currency could become illegal, as could transferring funds out of the country to buy gold, if it were outlawed here.

Increased taxes, currency controls and outlawing the ownership of precious metals are just some of the potential consequences that could emanate from a government that will soon wake from a spending binge the likes of which has never been seen before. And when the enormity of the damage they will have created starts to dawn on them and starts to dawn on the rest of the country, threatening their House or Senate seats, they will turn on the wealthy like machines from *The Matrix*, seeking income for the government in ways that all such governments have done in ages past—ways we have detailed above.

It is difficult to say it more succinctly or bluntly than was done in the highly regarded Casey Report earlier this year:

> Your government considers you a national resource to be exploited. If you don't get your money out of the country before the government gets your money out of you, you're an idiot, and you're going to get what you deserve.[15]

As the U.S. government deficits continue to roll forward and tax revenues continue to fall, it is a foregone conclusion that not only will taxes rise (forget the President's campaign promises; the idea that you can drive the government into more than a trillion dollars of debt every year and not raise taxes is a cruel joke) but the government will also seek new and "clever" ways to come after your assets.

You may blow this off as alarmist, conspiratorial, or just plain wrong. But, without getting dramatic or overly "serious" here, I suggest that you ignore this data at your peril.

Suggestions on what to do about this situation, both personally and politically, are detailed in the next article.

6
The Financial Crisis:
What You Can Do About It

November 2009

I have said it a number of times that there has been a coup d'état.

I'm not talking about Honduras. I'm talking about Wall Street, London, and Basel, Switzerland, and the fact that we are in the midst of a global financial coup instigated by a *Clockwork Orange* gang of international bankers.

The economic bloodletting has abated for now—at least the media's promotion of it has. In its place the media fawns on the very people who caused this crisis as they move forward to secure total global economic control. The carefully orchestrated spin is now designed to create acceptance of their "restructuring" of the international financial system in order to ensure this can never happen again.

Yes, I know, it sounds like an outtake from *Conspiracy Theory*, but I'm not Mel Gibson and you're not Julia Roberts. And this is not a screenplay.

Whether or not you accept the idea that the financial crisis was created for the purpose of replacing the United States and the U.S. dollar as the stable point in international finance with a global financial dictator and a new world currency, this scenario—set forth in our prior articles—is now in full swing.

This from the G-20 meeting in Pittsburg, September 26, 2009:

G-20 leaders push global economic reforms Friday

PITTSBURGH —

. . . The Pittsburgh meeting marked the third G-20 leaders summit in less than a year as the countries continued to grapple with a debilitating downturn that has resulted in millions of unemployed around the world, the loss of trillions of dollars in wealth and massive amounts of government stimulus spending designed to jump-start economic growth. . . .

"We are not going to walk away from the greatest economic crisis since the Great Depression and leave unchanged and leave in place the tragic vulnerabilities that caused this crisis," Treasury Secretary Timothy Geithner told reporters. . . .

Geithner said the G-20 countries had reached a consensus on the 'basic outline' of a proposal to limit bankers' compensation by the end of this year.

He said it would involve setting separate standards in each of the countries and would be overseen by the Financial Stability Board, an international group of central bankers, finance ministers and regulators that has representation from all the G-20 nations. (Emphasis mine.)[1]

While Geithner & Company are quietly empowering the Financial Stability Board (FSB), the United States and every other industrialized nation on earth are gushing money into their economies as if the printing presses were broken water mains.

The SDR

And just to make sure the planet drowns in the stuff, the International Monetary Fund (IMF) just announced (September 2009) that they had created $250 billion worth of SDRs and are going to spread them around the planet like a monetary Johnny Appleseed.[2]

SDR stands for "Special Drawing Rights." This is a currency that has been created by the IMF out of . . . eh . . . thin air. They say it is money and it is.

The SDR is "backed" by the dollar and the euro. These, in turn, are backed by . . . the same thin air. The IMF can create the stuff in unlimited quantities with digital alchemy, which amounts to simply adding zeros on a computer screen to suit the appetites of those countries dining at the IMF's table.

The CIA

But here's an interesting little secret: it wasn't really the IMF that created SDRs. A recently declassified CIA document makes clear that the fiscal geniuses at Langley did. In a secretly classified memo dated December 9, 1965, the agency discusses manipulating the gold market with central banks and the need for more "liquidity" because of the dollar's perceived weakness at the time. A section of the memo is quoted here. Take special note of the last sentence.

SECRET

Increasing liquidity.

Trade won't be able to grow, and the system will remain vulnerable to speculation unless there is regular growth in the international money supply.

Gold can't provide the needed increase: industrial and speculative demand is too high. U.S. payment deficits can't either: foreigners are unwilling to hold more dollars when we run large deficits and unable to increase net reserves by accumulating dollars when our deficits are small.

Our strategy is to supplement gold and dollars with a new international asset, Special Drawing Rights (SDR).[3]

There were too many dollars in circulation and for-eign governments that were holding dollars in reserve were considering turning theirs in for gold at the time. The CIA was trying to head off a run on Fort Knox by foreign governments.

Nixon Slams the Gold Window Shut

You see, until 1971, the U.S. dollar was pegged to gold at $35 an ounce. In other words, any foreign govern-ment (but not U.S. citizens) could turn their dollars in for gold—every $35 would get them an ounce of gold. When the costs of the Korean War and the Vietnam War turned our economy into a debtor nation (having to borrow to pay bills), we printed more dollars than there was gold to cover them.[4] Other nations knew this and grew concerned about their ability to receive gold in exchange for their dollars. In fact, French President Charles de Gaulle started cashing in France's green-backs for the real deal. To head off a run on our bul-lion, in 1971 Richard Nixon closed the "gold window."[5]

Without the dollar being tied to a physical com-modity, the Federal Reserve Bank had free license to print away.

As you know by now, the Federal Reserve Bank is a private corporation. The shareholders of the Fed are the large multinational banks, many of which are head-quartered in New York.

The Fed's real purpose is to create money in order

to lend it to the United States government. Given that it is a private corporation, the Fed's money is basically a corporate currency. At its core, it's no different than if Microsoft started to print bank notes that Congress designated as legal tender for the exchange of goods and services.

Think about that; it's corporate money. Pull a $5 bill out or your pocket/purse and you will see that it is labeled "Federal Reserve Note."

When the government spends more than it takes in, it must borrow the difference. The Fed prints up dead presidents and lends them to Sam (it's mostly digital money these days). And, of course, they charge interest on the money they loan, so it is in their interest for the country to spend more than it takes in.

Wars and Deficits

One of the primary reasons that a country goes in debt is to finance a war. Wars are costly. They create deficits, which require borrowing—from the Fed.

If there isn't a war, someone can simply start one:

March 10, 1964:
A secretly installed White House tape recorder is running.

President Johnson is on the phone with Secretary of Defense Robert McNamara regarding Vietnam:

"We need somebody over there that can get us some better

plans than we got. . .

"What I want is somebody that can lay up some plans to trap these guys . . . and whoop the hell out of 'em. Kill some of 'em. That's what I want to do."

McNamara:

"I'll try to bring something back that will meet that objective."[6]

August 4, 1964:

President Johnson goes before Congress claiming that U.S. ships have been attacked in the Gulf of Tonkin by North Vietnamese gunships. He seeks a joint resolution from Congress expressing support for all necessary action to protect our armed forces and to assist the nations in the region.[7]

On August 7, 1964, Congress passes joint resolution H.J. RES 1145, the Gulf of Tonkin Resolution, which gives President Johnson blanket authority to increase U.S. involvement in the war between North and South Vietnam.

Johnson and McNamara unleash the dogs of war. Dogs which cost the government $200 billion in 1974 dollars ($686 billion in 2008 dollars).

McNamara and the National Security Agency later admit that no such attack in the Gulf of Tonkin ever occurred.[8]

Isn't that special?

Now why in the world would the government create a war that didn't exist? I mean, who would benefit from such a thing?

Not American servicemen, fifty-eight thousand of whom lost their lives. Not America itself—the war tore the country apart. Not the Vietnamese people, 1.4 million of whom died, many incinerated by napalm. (We love you, Bob.)

But the owners of the Fed, the New York bankers who are always willing to, you know, extend a helping hand and lend some of their monopoly money to a needy Uncle—these guys got bloody rich when the government had to borrow billions to finance the war.

The outstanding national debt of the United States is about $13 trillion as of the writing of this book. The Fed doesn't own it all: China and Japan have some, as do others. The government pays out $452,000,000—half a trillion—a year in interest on the national debt. They get the money to pay the interest (and other expenses such as war and welfare) from income taxes made possible by the Sixteenth Amendment.

This is what my old man would have called "a killer deal."

Fiat Currencies

For the last several years, budget deficits (shortfalls) have been running a few hundred billion a year. Not good. But this year (2009), the deficit (outgo over income) will be $1.4 trillion. That means that the Fed's printing presses are burning rubber. In addition to the U.S., virtually every industrial nation on earth has gone to the presses in some fanatical jihad of liquidity.

What does this mean—with the IMF printing up $250 billion of SDRs and the governments of the world having their own fiat printing parties? It means that currencies are going to get less valuable and commodities will become more valuable.

Here is a definition of *fiat currency*. (I have taken *Wikipedia*'s definition and edited it for simplicity and am solely responsible for the content.)

Fiat money is money declared by a government to be legal tender. The term derives from the Latin *fiat*, meaning "let it be done." Fiat money achieves value because a government accepts it in payment of taxes and says it can be used within the country as a "tender" (offering) to pay all debts. In effect, this allows it to be used to buy goods and services and to pay tax. Where fiat money is used as currency, the term fiat currency is used. The most widely held reserve currency, the U.S. dollar, is a *fiat* currency, as are other widely held currencies like the Euro, Pound Sterling, and the Yuan.

In short, fiat currency is paper money sanctioned by a government. What stands behind the currency is the "full faith and credit" of the government, not gold or silver or any physical goods or services.

All of which leads us to the question, what does one do when fiat currencies are spreading like a plague of locusts?

When the government finishes their spending binge and wakes up to their eye-watering fiscal hangover, they will turn inward with a vengeance, seeking to filch money from every nook and cranny of the U.S. population.

When they do that, you need to be prepared. The following are my suggestions. They are based on thirty years of working in the area of banking, finance, credit and investment. Yet they are no more or less than my opinions. I have no crystal ball and offer no guarantees. What I do offer is the best advice I can, based on the data I have to hand.

Solutions

That said, here goes.

Precious Metals

When fiat currencies are debased, people turn to precious metals.

Why?

For one, they have intrinsic value. There is something almost magical about them. They have been prized and admired by people the world over for thousands of years. They have been used for everything from jewelry and crowns to tombs and offerings to the gods—a gold band symbolizes a marriage and pharaohs were buried in gold coffins. In modern day, both gold and silver have commercial and industrial uses.

And both have been used as money for eons. In 700 BC, Mesopotamian merchants used silver as a form of exchange. The Greek drachma, the Roman denarius and the British pound sterling all used silver in the creation of their money. Gold, too, was used to coin money hundreds of years before the time of Christ. Its use as the primary medium of monetary exchange has carried forward through time well into the twentieth century.

It was in 1933 that the U.S. government banned the ownership of gold. Still, dimes, quarters and halves contained 90 percent silver up until 1964, after which time the government ceased the practice.

Both metals also have extensive commercial and industrial uses: silver in photography, batteries, electronics, solar energy and water purification, to name a few. Gold is used in nanotechnology, electronics, dentistry, rocket engines, as well as watches and pens, to name a few more.

In short, man's fascination with gold and silver's decorative applications, their more recent industrial applications, as well as their use as money dates back thousands of years and is not about to change.

So when things get unstable in the world of finance, when fiat currencies are pouring off the presses in a blizzard of fiscal confetti, people turn to precious metals— gold and silver (and, to a lesser degree, platinum).

I have promoted the ownership of gold and silver since gold was under $300 an ounce and silver was $4.00 an ounce. As I write this, they are currently trading at $1,046 and $17.57, respectively.

These are handsome appreciations over a period of a few years, and there are those who believe gold and silver have run their course. I just finished reading a newsletter by one prognosticator who is convinced that the bull market* in precious metals is over. Perhaps he's right. Those who think the bull market in precious metals has run its course use government statistics to show that inflation is under control. But no one falsifies statistics like politicians. And even if the figures are correct, I think these metals markets have a long way to run.

Governments are still spraying dollars (or pounds or yen or yuan or euros) into their economies like some fiscal Agent Orange. And the IMF is engaged in distributing its SDR party favors cited above.

Inflation and Deflation

When the amount of money in circulation exceeds the goods and services available, the result is an economic illness called inflation.

Inflation is simply more money in circulation than there are goods and services to purchase. The money "competes" for the goods.

If you were, say, in a classroom and you had an orange to sell and every kid in the class had $10, the

---

* Bull market—When people are confident prices will go up they are "bullish." When think they will go down they are a "bear."

money would "compete" for the purchase of the orange, which would probably sell for $10.

But what if every kid in the classroom had $100? What would happen to the price of the orange?

This is called inflation.

Deflation is just the opposite. What if the kids in our classroom each had a buck?

This is not the rocket science that Harvard Business School professors would have you believe.

So with the amount of money in circulation reaching stratospheric levels (see following chart), why is the consumer price index hibernating like a grizzly in February?

The answer comes from Nobel Laureate Milton Friedman who, in 1972, found that there was a lag of over a year before an expanded money supply caused a noticeable effect on inflation and interest rates.[10] This is supported in a recent study by two economists at the Bank of England—Nicoletta Batini and Edward Nelson—who analyzed U.S. and UK money growth rates, inflation and interest rates from 1953 to 2001.[11]

They found the same correlation. Another study at the European Central Bank documented an eighteen-month lag.

The U.S. government started pouring money into the economy in the fourth quarter of 2008 and is continuing to do so. The Europeans followed a bit later. All of which is to say that if Friedman and the others are correct, inflation should become manifest around the summer of 2010.

For all of the above reasons, I recommend that people place some of their reserve assets into precious metals. My recommendation is that 20–25 percent be in precious metals—for the adventurous, even more.

There is no magic to this figure. Some people will be comfortable with a smaller percentage; others will do more. But having some assets in gold and silver in times like these is something with which Yoda would agree.

What to Buy?

Silver

I favor silver. I recommend an allocation of about 70 percent silver, 30 percent gold. There are several reasons for this. First of all, it's cheaper. If you had

$10,000 to invest today, you could buy 569 ounces of silver, but only 10 ounces of gold (9½ really). Now of course gold moves (appreciates and depreciates) in dollars and silver in cents, but let's look at a little history.

When gold hit its peak thirty years ago, it topped out at $850 an ounce. Today, it is trading at about $1,050.

When gold hit $850, silver peaked at $50 an ounce. But today, silver is trading a bit over $17. You think it may have some room to the upside?

There are other factors involved, but the bottom line is, I think you have much better upside potential with silver.

Silver can be purchased in a number of different forms. If you are buying silver strictly for investment purposes, with no thought to the use of silver for money or exchange, then one can buy bullion in 10 oz, 100 oz or 1,000 oz bars.

Junk Silver

The breakdown of the silver would depend on how much one has to spend. If you have $12,000 (given today's prices) I would recommend a bag of "junk" silver. Junk silver is pre-1965 dimes, quarters, and halves.

Silver coins prior to 1965 were made from 90 percent silver. So they appreciate with the silver market and are legal currency of the United States. They protect against inflation and serve as a potential source of currency if the financial system and/or the economy completely collapse. If you have a few hundred thousand to invest, get two or three bags.

Silver Eagles

Several governments mint gold and silver coins. In addition to the United States—Canada, Australia, China, Mexico, and Austria are well-known manufacturers of such coins.

Buying one-ounce silver coins is an excellent second tier to one's silver portfolio. I recommend that you buy the one-ounce silver coin of the country in which you live if they mint one.

If you live in America, the name of the one-ounce coin minted by the U.S. government is the Silver Eagle. These are not official currency—they aren't government-sanctioned money. But in hard times, they would very likely serve as an excellent medium of exchange.

Silver Eagles normally sell for about 10 percent over the spot price* of silver. As I write this, silver eagles are selling for about $18 a piece. So, 1,000 eagles would be $18,000—and so forth.

There are also local and regional companies that mint one-ounce silver coins. They are almost always priced for less than the Eagles. This simply has to do with the trust factor. If you had to exchange a couple

---

* Spot price—Today's price, as opposed to a forward price or future price.

of silver coins for a tank of gas, the coins minted by the U.S. government are more likely to be accepted than those from a local mint.

Given this fact, it makes sense to pay the slight premium for the coins minted by the government.

The third part of the silver portfolio should be silver bars. Again, the amount depends on how much you are intending to invest, but 99 percent pure silver bars are sold in 10 oz, 100 oz and 1,000 oz sizes.

These are called bullion bars and tend to be purchased more for the purpose of straight investment than the ability to use them in times of economic crisis.

Gold

Like silver, gold bullion can be purchased in the form of bars and coins. Both are sold in multiple sizes. For instance, gold coins are sold in 1 oz, $^1/_2$ oz, $^1/_4$ oz and $^1/_{10}$ oz. While there is a premium for the smaller-sized coins (and the premium is usually higher the smaller the size), I recommend having some of these smaller sizes in your portfolio.

The reason is, if things get financially chaotic—I'm not saying they will, but it is not out of the question—then having some smaller denominations can provide a better medium of exchange. In other words, it would be easier to, say, pay for the family's groceries using a $^1/_{10}$ oz gold coin (currently \$142) than a 1 oz. coin (currently \$1,143).

One-ounce gold coins are the most common and are frequently traded. Gold bars come in a wide variety of sizes: 1 oz., 10 oz., 100 oz., 400 oz., and more.

Again, I recommend some fractional gold coins for potential use for trade and barter in case things become financially chaotic. In times such as those, fiat currency becomes essentially worthless and gold and silver coins become "the coin of the realm."

Model Portfolio

Here's an example of a "model portfolio," if someone had $100,000 to invest in precious metals today. I use that figure because it is round. If you have less to invest (or more), you can proportion it accordingly. This portfolio is at today's prices and the price of metals will almost certainly be different when you are reading this book.

Moreover, these recommendations are not set in stone. They are simply how I look at these markets. Many people favor gold more strongly than I do, while others are not interested in coins and prefer bullion bars, which they buy strictly for investment purposes.

To repeat, I place considerable value on gold and silver coins as potential backup "currency" should the wheels totally come off the economic wagon.

That said, I feel this kind of allotment would serve people well using the $100,000 model.

2 bags of "junk" silver	$ 26,000
750 Silver Eagles	$ 14,798
50 x 10 oz. silver bars	$ 9,200
10 x 100 oz. silver bars	$ 18,330
Total silver	$ 68,328
10 x $1/10$ oz. gold coins	$ 1,410
10 x ¼ oz. gold coins	$ 2,900
9 x ½ oz. gold coins	$ 5,193
10 x 1 oz. Gold Eagles	$ 11,410
1 x 10 oz. gold bar	$ 10,662
Total gold	$ 31,575
Total	$ 99,903

Leaving you a few bucks for shipping.

Where to Buy?

It is a sign of the times that there seem to be more precious metals dealers than car dealerships these days. So there is no shortage of places to shop for your precious metals.

I use the word "shop" advisedly because precious metals prices can vary widely. Dealers usually charge a certain percent over the spot price of the metal for coins or bars. This percentage varies from dealer to dealer. The big houses tend to be competitive, but there is no guarantee of that.

The markup from the spot price can run from 3 percent to 4.5 percent on a single Gold Eagle to 11 percent plus for a single Silver Eagle. And these are just ballpark numbers taken from a few key sites. Moreover, these percentages diminish rapidly as the volume and the amount of the purchase increase.

The bottom line is you need to shop the pricing. And in doing so, you need to contact the prospective dealers on the same day to get comparative pricing. Precious metals markets can move by the minute. However, dealers generally lock in prices for one trading day (though not always, so be sure to check).

And while price is always important, there are other factors involved—the foremost of which is to deal with a well established, trusted precious metals dealer. Many of the top firms have been around for decades. It is hard to stay in business that long, particularly in the precious metals business, if you are not honest and trustworthy. Length of time in business is certainly not a guarantee, but it is a good gauge.

You also want to make sure, if you have the metals shipped, that the package is insured, and if they charge for shipping, how much.

I use Colorado Gold for myself and my clients (www.

coloradogold.com) 1-888-786-8822. The owner's name is Don Stott, who has been a precious metals broker for more than thirty years. I have found him to be trustworthy in all of my dealings with him.

Moreover, he has the best prices for precious metals that I can find. This doesn't mean you couldn't search and find someone lower. This isn't a "price guarantee" for Colorado Gold. It is just a statement of my experience. Don charges 1.5 percent for his brokerage services. For orders over $35,000 he charges 1 percent including insured shipping, and ¾ percent including insured shipping for orders over $75,000. By all means, do your own research. These are simply people I have used and with whom I have had good experience.

Storage

There are several ways to buy and store precious metals. The first is to have the metals shipped to your home and put in a safe. Even if the order is too large for home delivery, I recommend that you take delivery of some gold and silver coins, as these take up very little room and it may be important to have them close to hand at some point.

If you are only going to take partial delivery of the order and want the rest stored, then you need a facility that specializes in precious metals storage—not your bank safe-deposit box, as "bank holidays" (banks closing for some period of time) are a very real prospect for the financial industry in the United States in the years to come. I would not recommend storing your metals with your dealer. That is asking for trouble.

Some of the larger precious metals dealers have relationships to which they can refer you or deliver your metals. Needless to say, the selection of a company to store your metals is extremely important. Ideally, you should go and physically inspect the facility.

If your dealer does not provide you with a referral, you have to find one. I know that Brinks offers precious metals storage at some of its locations. But the best place for storage appears to be a facility in Delaware called Delaware Depository.

Delaware Depository

I have not used them nor have I been there, so please do your own due diligence on any metals storage facility you are considering. However, from the looks of their services and their licensing, they appear to be an excellent choice. (www.delawaredepository.com)

There are a couple of other options that are worthy of mention.

GoldMoney

One is GoldMoney (www.goldmoney.com). This is from their website:

GoldMoney® enables you to hold gold, silver & platinum that is fully insured and stored securely in specialised bullion vaults in Zurich and London. All metal is owned directly by you with no counterparty risk!

I have yet to personally use them, though multiple people have recommended them. They provide some unique services. Go to the site and check them out.

Perth Mint

Another alternative if you do not want to store your metals at home is The Perth Mint (www.perthmint.com). The Perth Mint was founded in 1899 and is owned by the government of Western Australia. They have a unique, highly regarded program of storing precious metals that you buy from them and providing you with a widely recognized "Perth Mint Certificate." The mint has a handful of dealers in key jurisdictions around the world.

This brief summary is from their website (www.Perthmint.com):

The Perth Mint has a strong reputation for excellence and innovation and now offers a variety of different methods of precious metal investment to cater for individual investor needs.

Investors who do not want the inconvenience and risk of storing their precious metals can take advantage of the investment products that The Perth Mint has developed. These products allow investors to buy gold, silver and platinum via its Certificate and Depository programs. . .

Alternatively, The Perth Mint manufactures a wide range of bullion coins and bullion bars for those who prefer to store physical precious metal themselves. Information on these products can be accessed by clicking on any one of the four menu choices above. If you have any questions about The Perth Mint's investment products or how to invest in gold, silver and platinum.

Check it out. The Perth Mint is one of the world's most enduring institutions of precious metals.

In short, you can buy yourself a good safe and take personal delivery of your metals; you can have your metals stored at a professional precious metals storage facility; you can purchase from and have your metals stored in a place like The Perth Mint, or any combination thereof.

Foreign Currencies

Remember, no national currency is backed by gold today. The strength of a currency, then, is really a reflection of the economic health and productivity of the country issuing it. The dollar's swan dive over the last couple of years is a reflection of America's massive budget deficits, trade imbalances and the corresponding fall from economic grace. There was at time, not so long ago, when the American economy was the envy of the world and the greenback was "as good as gold."

This is no longer the case.

The strongest major economy on the planet today is that of the PRC—People's Republic of China. And this is why I recommend diversifying some of one's assets into the yuan (also referred to as the renminbi or RMB). Am I a fan of the government of mainland China? I am not. But in one of the great demonstrations of political-economic irony, the commissars at the Chinese Communist Party have turned the Chinese economy into a quasi–free market system that is now the most productive on the planet. Go figure. But that productivity provides an underlying natural strength to the yuan.

Make no mistake. China has been hurt by the global depression. But this has been like Ray Robinson landing a punishing uppercut to Jake "Raging Bull" LaMotta in the final round of their last encounter (Sugar Ray won four of the five in what are arguable the greatest middleweight fights of all time; Robinson landed a hail of punches in the last round, but LaMotta never went down), not like Buster Douglas's historic knockout of "Iron Mike" Tyson in Tokyo in 1990.

And if you are not a fight fan or find the boxing metaphors on the far side of tortured, I think you get the picture: China has taken a hit, but it is still on its feet and producing, while the finance ministers of the rest of the world's economies gather at G-20 meetings and dine on platitudes while issuing pretentious calls for "quantitative easing" (means print more money).

Yuan/RMB deposit accounts can be opened at Everbank. Everbank (www.everbank.com) is a bank head-quartered in Florida. They take deposits in U.S. dollars but you can also open accounts in several foreign currencies. This enables you to diversify some assets into other currencies that hopefully will stand up more strongly than the dollar.

This bank's deposits, even those in foreign currencies, are insured by the U.S. government for $250,000 per account holder. (Note: This insurance was increased from $100,000 to $250,000 last year but is set to revert to $100,000 on January 1, 2014. This lowering of coverage does not apply to IRAs and other certain retirement accounts, which will remain at $250,000 per depositor.)

However, if you are married, you can actually get coverage for up to $1,000,000. Here's how.

You open an account in your name. It is covered

for $250,000. Your spouse opens an account is his/her name. It is covered for $250,000. You open a joint account in both names and each of you is covered for an additional $250,000.[12]

For further currency diversification and to protect against a declining dollar, one could consider the Norwegian krone. Yes, I know, it's probably not sitting at the top of your investment radar screen. But these folks run one of the most fiscally responsible governments on the planet. Many do not know that Norway is the third largest exporter of oil on the planet (tons of the stuff off their coast in the North Sea) and utilizes its $1.5 billion dollars a week in oil revenues to keep this country as economically strong as their Viking ancestors.

The Chicago Tribune reported on this phenomenon in November, 2007:

OSLO, Norway — If you wanted to design a small, 21st-century nation from scratch, combining outrageous good fortune with virtue, you'd probably come up with something like Norway.

With a per capita income of $65,509, Norway ranks second only to super-rich Luxembourg. Much of the wealth derives from North Sea oil, but Norwegians have barely touched a penny of it, instead putting more than $350 billion into an investment fund for future generations.[13]

Norway numbers:

Per capita income: $65,509 (second only to Luxembourg)

Health-care services: Available to all of its 4.6 million people, with the cap on out-of-pocket expenses at $200 a year.

Maternity leave: Working women get a year off at 80 percent pay.

Oil exports: The world's third largest after Saudi Arabia and Russia. Its 2.9 million barrels a day bring in roughly $1.8 billion a week (at $96 a barrel).[14]

Norway has a 10 percent budget *surplus*. This compared to the 40 percent, $1.4 trillion budget deficit in the U.S. But that is just the beginning because the fiscal brain trust in the White House and Congress are now calling for a "second stimulus," a trillion-dollar health care plan and multibillion-dollar extensions of unemployment insurance.

These people are smoking something. The country is in the midst of an economic meltdown and they're like . . .

Nancy to Harry:
"Dude, I know, let's keep paying people not to work."

Harry:
"Awesome. Let me check with the O man, but I know he'll be down with this."

For whatever reason, the government of Norway is not afflicted by BDD—budget deficit disorder—the inability to spend less than you take in. All of which is to say that the Norwegian krone is backed by hundreds of billions a year in oil revenue and that rarest of organizations, a fiscally responsible government.

Krone deposits are also available at Everbank.

An Offshore Solution

Growing numbers of people are moving assets offshore into gold, silver, and stronger currencies such as the Norwegian Krone and the Chinese Yuan. Seeing the coming tsunami of government debt and inflation and potential confiscation of personal wealth, many are turning to offshore jurisdictions that provide privacy and outstanding asset protection.

Government taxing authorities would love to have people believe that moving assets offshore is somehow immoral or even illegal. Nothing could be further from the truth.

According to the U.S. Government Accountability Office, 83 of the nation's 100 largest corporations, including world-class brands such as General Motors, Pepsi, News Corp and Wells Fargo, had subsidiaries in offshore tax havens in 2007. In fact, hundreds of thousands of offshore entities—corporations and foundations—operate legally in tax haven jurisdictions from Panama to Liechtenstein, from the British Virgin Islands (BVI) to Hong Kong.

Offshore corporations, foundations and trusts can usually be set up for nominal amounts and enable those creating them to move some of their assets out of dollars and out of the reach of fiscally irresponsible, avaricious governments. Offshore entities enable those creating them to not only protect their assets from the world's most litigious society but also give them access to world markets that are not available in the United States. Offshore entities also can help facilitate the movement of currency or capital should the U.S. impose currency controls or seek to confiscate precious metals holdings.

There are many companies that provide these services. However, I decided to research this area myself. After considerable study and enough international travel to make my air miles account pregnant with upgrades, I set up a site to help people that were considering this strategy at www.offshorefinancialsolutions.com.

Some words of caution: Do not set up an offshore entity to evade taxes. It is against the law. Panamanian foundations, for instance, are terrific for asset protection; they are wonderful estate planning tools, and they provide access to foreign currency, securities, and commodities markets.

But these activities should be undertaken to protect your assets and give you access to foreign investment markets and freedom of movement of your capital—not for tax evasion. U.S. citizens are required to report offshore accounts and income they earn from anywhere in the world, so our strongest possible advice is that you obey the laws of your country regarding tax matters.

That said, there are some selected legal tax advantages in conducting business offshore. To understand the tax rules for conducting business or investment activities offshore, you should have the advice of a top offshore tax accountant. One CPA who specializes in this area is Vernon Jacobs. His website is www.vernonjacobs.com. He offers offshore tax advice to other CPAs, lawyers, and individuals, as well as access to several books he has written on the subject.

You should also be aware that if you open up offshore accounts (e.g., deposit accounts, brokerage accounts) you must report their existence on your federal income tax return. One of Vernon Jacobs' books covers this topic in considerable detail.

But regardless of where you might have this done, bear in mind that Uncle is broke. He's more than broke, he's short more than a trillion this year with projections for the same well into the future, and I think you would be wise to consider moving some of your assets offshore and out of U.S. dollars.

Summary

Financial Solutions

In summary, we recommend that the following as long as you bear in mind that conditions change and markets change. And while these recommendations are based on the best advice I can provide, they are also based on current conditions and prevailing market factors. That said,

1. Approximately 25 percent of your reserves be placed in precious metals;

2. About 70 percent of those metals should be in silver and 30 percent in gold;

3. Another 10 –15 percent be placed in foreign currencies—specifically, the Chinese yuan (RMB) and the Norwegian krone;

4. The balance should be kept liquid in cash and short-term Treasury bills so that you can take advantage of opportunities that will become available as economies continue to deteriorate.

Political Solutions

Political solutions are detailed in the first two articles, "Behind the Wizard's Curtain", and "Hitler's Bank Goes Global", but I want to reiterate and expand upon them here one last time. Because if we are ever going to truly take control of global financial matters in a way that benefits people and not bankers, there are two vital things that need to be done.

One

In the short term members of Congress and Members of the Parliaments of the G-20 nations should insist that a representative legislative body be set up at international level that has full oversight and corrective powers over the FSB and similar international financial and trade organizations. This would automatically ensure that national central banks would be subject to the full oversight and corrective powers of duly constituted legislative bodies.

In the U.S. a body like the FSB must be confirmed either by treaty or Congressional Executive Agreement (though they seem unaware of this fact as of this writing.). This treaty or Congressional Executive Agreement would serve as a vehicle to create a legislative oversight and enforcement body over the FSB.

In the case of inaction by the Executive branch (which has been the case to date), this may require the introduction of formal legislation. I outline how to do that in "Hitler's Bank Goes Global".

It is important to note here that other member countries have similar mechanisms. Now, more than ever, citizens must start paying close attention to the machinations of unelected international financial bodies or they will find themselves operating at the effect of such bodies with no real remedy to hand.

Challenging to be sure, but the alternative opens the door to an Orwellian world that has no place for the exercise of individual liberty. On the other hand, creating this structure will help guarantee personal freedom for all people.

Two

Once that is done the creation of an international monetary system that is based on property and production would have to be insisted upon.

In other words a monetary system that is not based on fiat or an unworkable commodity, such as gold, but on what money actually represents and that is all of the production (goods and services) and property value (real estate and land value) of nations.

For example, a realistic assessment of the country's Gross Domestic Product (GDP) and property value would yield and amount—say $100 billion. The country's national bank would ensure that was the amount of currency in circulation. They couldn't print more or less than that amount, and that would mean no inflation, no deflation, just sufficient money to buy what was available to buy.

This would guarantee that the economy is based on

stable and real economic measures. It would be based on the most fundamental definitions of inflation and deflation. Inflation being the result of more money than goods and deflation being more goods than money, and financial matters would be maintained accordingly.

Based on this system each state or country would be allocated, as its money, the exact value of its property, real or personal, as well as its current value of production. The currency would be issued by an international body which could be the IMF, but only once it is irrevocably and unalterably under the oversight and corrective powers of a legislative body and bound by this monetary system precluding private, corporate and political abuse.

In other words all branches of government would be bound by the formula described above and, thus, neither the executive, legislative or banking organization could institute policies that are debt-based.

Once in place, each year, by careful survey the extant funds in a country or state would be increased or decreased to match its productivity on the premise that money must exist to purchase that which exists to be purchased.

This would make the pursuit of happiness a reality for all people and make the American dream a global reality.

This would result in actual free trade and resolve balance of payment problems, as the currency would be interchangeable, all having the same value. Free trade would also include free trade of oil. It would allow for oil exploration that is unfettered by unsustainable monetary policy. It would end currency manipulation, artificial oil scarcity and eliminate the most prevalent cause for current wars, which aside from human death and misery create considerable environmental damage. It would also, obviously, abolish carbon credits. In short it would create an abundance of energy and a future of productivity in which all life would be able to prosper.

I don't take pleasure or joy in detailing the economic takeover of the planet by a gang of pinstriped hoods. But these are not normal times and if one is informed, he can take the appropriate steps to protect himself and his family and what assets he may have put away for the proverbial rainy day.

I hope you find these suggestions helpful. And remember to keep your powder dry.

7
Cyprus and the Global Banking Mafia

When Alexander the Great ruled Cyprus, the Mediterranean island tucked into the underbelly of Turkey like a fetus in the geo-political womb, he took control of the island's currency by removing the images of the local kings on the coins and replace them with his own.

Alexander's military genius was often accompanied by a savage brutality. But his rule of Cyprus, where the local kings wisely embraced him as a homie and jumped on the "Alexander is Conquering the World" crusade, was essentially economic and political.

The Organized Crime Family of Global Finance

The modern day pretenders to world domination, the international bankers, or "The Troika" as they are known in Europe, have been much more brutal in their suppression of the banking system and economy of Cyprus. But then their plans reached much farther than this Mediterranean tax haven awash with deposits from retired KGB capitalists and modern day Russian Oligarchs (deposits from Russians made up $20 billion of the $68 billion in bank accounts on Cyprus).

The Troika is the name given to the European

branch of the organized crime family in charge of managing the European Financial Crisis. It is made up of the IMF, the European Central Bank (ECB) and the European Commission (the governing body of the European Union).

Is it possible that the banking crisis on this small, island nation halfway around the world could affect the deposit accounts in the United States?

In ways you could hardly imagine.

Cyprus was a pilot—a test—of a much larger, global agenda. It reads like a script from a Bond movie.

If only it were fiction...

Your deposit accounts in U.S. banks are not what you think they are. But I am getting ahead of myself; the story starts on Cyprus.

The two largest banks in Cyprus, the Bank of Cyprus and Laiki Bank, had previously purchased bonds from the land of Pericles—no surprise as 78% of the population of Cyprus is of Greek heritage.

When Greece defaulted on its IOUs in February of 2012, these banks suffered devastating losses. They were kept alive by injections from the European Central Bank (the Fed for the EU), who had threatened to pull the needle unless the Cypriot government and the banks agreed to a bailout.

Like all Mafia agreements, it was a deal Cyprus could not refuse.

Had they not agreed, their dealer would have removed the needle from their banking system and they would have been thrown out of the EU, relegating them to the planet's financial leper colony currently populated solely by Iceland.

The Cypriot government caved. Here's what happened.

The Troika agreed to a 10 billion Euro ($12.8 billion dollar) bailout. But it's really a bail-in because depositors with more than 100,000 euros in the country's two largest banks got an eye-watering haircut totaling 5.8 billion euros.

There hasn't been a mass scalping like this since Sitting Bull hacked off Custer's curls along with the rest of the hapless members of the Seventh Cavalry at Little Big Horn.

In plain English, the depositors are going to eat a portion of the bank's loses.

Yum.

What Happened In Cyprus

Here are the details.

Laiki Bank, the country's second largest, is being closed. Accounts with 100,000 euros ($128,000) or less are being transferred to the Bank of Cyprus, the largest.

Accounts at Laiki with deposits in excess of 100,000 euros—a total of 4.2 billion euros—are being transferred to a "Bad Bank," which sounds like they are being sent to the principal's office. But transfer to a Bad Bank in Cyprus means they are being written off.

All of Laiki's bond holders and other creditors are also being sent to the principal's office from which they will not return. All the creditors, that is, except Laiki's 9 billion euro loan from the European Central Bank—that's being transferred to the Bank of Cyprus.

Isn't that special?

Depositors in the Bank of Cyprus with account balances in excess of 100,000 euros will have about 40% of the excess converted to stock in the bank.

How cool is that? Without even being asked, they are getting an investment in the bank's stock. The fact that the bank is bankrupt is...well, tough.

Another 20% of the excess is being put in a special non-interest bearing account that is subject to additional write off.

For example, if you had 500,000 euros in the Bank of Cyprus, about 160,000 has been converted to stock in the bank and another 80,000 has been snatched from your account and put into a non-interest bearing account which may be used for more of the bail-in.

Leaves you with 260,000 euros. The silver haired Marxists at the IMF refer to it as a "wealth tax". Karl is orgasmic.

This was the first time account holder's funds have been summarily taken from them to cover the failure of the bank in which the deposits were held.

But it won't be the last. Oh no, not by a long shot.

In Europe, Jeroen Dijsselbloem, the Dutch Finance Minister who helped structure the Cyprus bail-in, told reporters on March 25th that the Cyprus plan would be

"...the template for any future bank bailouts."

Financial markets roiled after the statement and Mario Draghi, the Darth Vaderish President of the European Central Bank, denied the report and publicly chastised Dijsselbloem, but this is clearly the unspun thinking of The Troika.

The Plan of the FDIC and the Bank of England

And it won't be the last if the FDIC and the Bank of England have anything to say about it.

You see, rather than being a one-time, extraordinary event, the handling of the Cyprus banking crisis was the opening gambit of a little known plan. That plan is to "Bail–in" bank failures of those that are deemed "Too big to fail" by **having the depositors cover a percentage of the bank's losses**.

Say what?

That's right. However, the term "Too big to fail" got some push back during the financial crisis of 2008-2009, and so the banking elite have resorted to their time-honored tactic of using terminology that is understood by...virtually no one.

Thus, the joint plan issued by the FDIC and the Bank of England on December 10, 2012 is not for banks that are too big to fail. No, no. It is for "Globally Active, Systemically Important, Financial Institutions", G-SIFIs for short.

They are no longer banks, they are G-SIFIs. Sounds

like something out of the Martian Chronicles.

Listen to the boys from the Bank of England and the FDIC:

"An efficient path for returning the sound operations of the G-SIFI to the private sector would be provided by exchanging or converting a sufficient amount of the unsecured debt from the original creditors of the failed company into equity."

In English, Comrade.

You probably think that when you deposit money in the bank, they are holding your funds for you.

Eh... Sorry.

Legally, once you give your money to the bank, they own your funds. The deposit is a bank liability—a debt—and you have become a creditor. Your deposit isn't secured by anything, so you are what is known as an unsecured creditor.

And equity? That's another name for ownership of a company or...stock.

So, let's read it again: returning the G-SIFI (the bank) to the private sector (the FDIC took over the bank when it failed. Now they are going to turn it private again.) would be provided by converting a sufficient amount of unsecured debt (deposits) into equity (stock).

The FDIC plan is to take some of your deposits and turn them into stock and recapitalize the bank. Moreover,

"No exception is indicated for 'insured deposits'

in the U.S., meaning those under $250,000, the deposits we thought were protected by FDIC insurance. This can hardly be an oversight, since it is the FDIC that is issuing the directive." http://www.counterpunch.org/2013/03/28/the-confiscation-scheme-planned-for-us-and-uk-depositors/

And where did this bizarre plan originate?

The Bank For International Settlements

The plan originates from the Financial Stability Board, a newly created entity that acts as a hit man for the Bank for International Settlements (BIS)—the bad boys of Basel, Switzerland.

Earlier in this book, I exposed the creation and purpose of the Financial Stability Board and turned an investigative spotlight on the BIS. If the European Central Bank, the IMF and the U.S. Federal Reserve are heads of the planet's financial crime families, the Bank for International Settlements is the Godfather and the Financial Stability Board, Luca Brasi.

On April 2, 2009, the members of the G-20 (a loose-knit organization of the central bankers and finance ministers of the twenty major industrialized nations) issued a communiqué that gave birth to what is no less than Big Brother in a three-piece suit.

Which means?

The communiqué announced the creation of the

all-too-Soviet-sounding Financial Stability Board (FSB).

The Financial Stability Board. Remember that name well, because they now have control of the planet's finances…and, when one peels the onion of the communiqué, control of much, much more.

The Bank for International Settlements (BIS), out of which the FSB operates… (is) Known as Hitler's bank, the Bank for International Settlements worked arm in arm with the Nazis, facilitating the transfer of gold from Nazi-occupied countries to the Reichsbank, and kept Germany's lines open to the international financial community during the Second World War.

The BIS is completely above the law.

It is like a sovereign state. Its personnel have diplomatic immunity for their persons and papers. No taxes are levied on the bank or the personnel's salaries. The grounds are sovereign, as are the buildings and offices. The Swiss government has no legal jurisdiction over the bank and no government agency or authority has oversight over its operations.

In a 2003 article titled "Controlling the World's Monetary System: The Bank for International Settlements," Joan Veon wrote:

"The BIS is where all of the world's central banks meet to analyze the global economy and determine what course of action they will take next to put more money in their pockets, since they control the amount of money in circulation and how much interest they are going to charge governments and banks for borrowing from them.... When you understand that the BIS pulls the strings of the world's monetary system, you then understand that they have the ability to create a financial boom or bust in a country. If that country is not doing what the money lenders want, then all they have to do is sell its currency."

So it is no surprise to find that the plan to use depositor's money to cover bank failures originated from the Financial Stability Board.

The pretense is that these august institutions are operating in the best interest of the public. What a joke.

The BIS and its minions, the European Central Bank, the IMF and the U.S. Fed, are run by bankers interested in protecting themselves and maintaining their financial control over the governments and economies of Earth.

Which leaves us where?

- The two largest banks in Cyprus were failing. In March of this year (2013), the IMF, the European Central Bank, and the European Union (known as The Troika) forced a "bail out" plan on the banks that included converting billions of euros of depositor's funds to bank stock.

- The depositors had no say in this as it turns out that bank deposits are actually owned by the bank, the depositors being unsecured creditors.

- It also turns out that this plan was not a unique, one-time solution, but the initial step of a strategic agenda, which was formally issued by the FDIC and the Bank of England on December 10, 2012.

- The FDIC / Bank of England plan originated from the Financial Stability Board, the newly created enforcer for the Bank for International Settlements, the planet's most powerful and controlling financial institution.

Derivatives

There is, however, one more piece of this puzzle that directly affects depositors of U.S. banks. An important piece.

To understand this aspect of the game, one must have a rudimentary understanding of Derivatives—a type of investment Warren Buffet has called Financial Weapons of Mass Destruction.

Derivatives are financial instruments that derive their value from some underlying asset.

The term was slammed into the public consciousness during the financial crisis of 2008–2009 among discussions of the infamous mortgage-backed securities.

Mortgages were packaged up and sold in bundles to banks and others. The actual mortgages were the underlying asset.

But mortgage-backed securities are not the boogie-man of international finance today—oh no.

Interest Rate Swaps

The entire planet is now mired in a vast interconnected Ponzi scheme of more than **$1.2 Quadrillion** dollars of derivatives, the majority of which (about 60%) are bets on the direction of interest rates.

That's right; about seven hundred trillion dollars of these derivatives are what are called interest rate swaps and are traded in a casino that is so vast even the people who built it have lost control.

Interest rate swaps are nothing more than bets on the direction of interest rates—will they rise or fall? An investment bank thinks rates will go up. Another bank thinks they will go down.

And they bet.

The bet is called a swap (they are swapping risk).

Those doing the betting are called counter-parties.

Once a bet is made, there are bets on that bet and bets on those bets and then bets on the bets of the bets, and today...stay with me...they make up a $700,000,000,000—seven hundred TRILLION dollar house of cards.

The figure is mind numbing.
How exposed are U.S. Banks?

Bank of New York Mellon: $1.375 Trillion in
    derivatives
State Street Financial: $1.390 Trillion in
    derivatives
Morgan Stanley: $1.722 Trillion in derivatives
Wells Fargo: $3.332 Trillion in derivatives
HSBC: $4.321 Trillion in derivatives
Goldman Sachs: $44.192 Trillion in derivatives
Bank of America: $50.135 Trillion in derivatives
Citibank: $52,102 Trillion in derivatives
JP Morgan Chase: $70,151 Trillion in derivatives
Total derivatives exposure of the nine biggest US
    banks: $228.72 Trillion http://demonocracy.
    info/infographics/usa/derivatives/bank_expo-
    sure.html

However, note that because there are bets on bets on
bets, many of the derivatives would cancel each other
out—the actual cash that is at risk is about 20% of the
face amount above or about $45 trillion (the entire
annual production of the U.S. economy is about $15
trillion).

Still, there was a piece of the derivative picture that
puzzled me. The biggest banks in the country, the guys
that own the Fed, are buried in trillions of dollars of
derivatives. The majority of the derivatives are interest rate swaps. Sooner or later interest rates are going

to rise, and when they do, many of the banks that own these swaps are going to get slaughtered.

But surely they know that. They may be evil, but they aren't stupid when it comes to their own survival.

And then the penny dropped.

The original article I read on this situation written by Ellen Brown (one of the few researchers who understands who and what the BIS is and does—www.ellenbrown.com) linked to another article that turned all the lights on. http://www.nakedcapitalism.com/2013/03/when-you-werent-looking-democrat-bank-stooges-launch-bills-to-permit-bailouts-deregulate-derivatives.html

> "In the US, depositors have actually been put in a worse position than Cyprus deposit-holders, at least if they are at the big banks that play in the derivatives casino. The regulators have turned a blind eye as banks use their depositories to fund derivatives exposures...(remember, depositors are unsecured creditors)... One big reason was that derivatives reforms made derivatives counterparties require collateral for any exposures, meaning they are secured creditors. The 2005 bankruptcy reforms made derivatives counter parties senior to unsecured lenders."

Remember the effect of the 2005 bankruptcy law revisions: derivatives counter parties are first in line, they get to grab the assets first and leave everyone else to scramble for crumbs.

You get the picture now: the Bank for International Settlements, through its Financial Stability Board created a strategy that failing banks (and those pregnant with the evil spawn of derivatives) could save themselves by taking some of their depositors funds and converting them to stock in the bank.

For example, Bank of America transferred its derivatives from its Merrill Lynch operation to its depository operation (the bank) in late 2011.

Ellen Brown states it quite clearly:

"The deposits are now subject to being wiped out by a major derivatives loss." http://www.counterpunch.org/2013/03/28/the-confiscation-scheme-planned-for-us-and-uk-depositors/

What To Do

1. In the first place, according to one source, the FDIC will have to get legislative approval for their plan.

"Congress would never approve such a law," you say. Really?

Take a look at a couple of corporate lobbying coups:

April 1, 2013, The Monsanto Protection Act, which President Obama signed into law this week, will strip judges of their constitutional mandate to protect consumer rights and the environment, while opening up the floodgates for the planting of new untested genetically engineered crops, endangering farmers, consumers and the environment. The result is that GMO crops will be able to evade any serious scientific or regulatory review. http://www.nationof-change.org/how-monsanto-protection-act-be-came-law-1364825964

Did you know that when the pharmaceutical industry muscled the Prescription Drug Benefit law through Congress a few years ago—a trillion dollar taxpayer gift to Big Pharma—which contains a provision that **prohibits** the government from negotiating the price they pay for drugs?

And, as the great Dave Barry says, "We are not making this up." http://www.ourfuture.org/makingsense/alert/2008083312/negotiate-prescription-drug-prices

And you have seen above how the banking industry managed to legislate derivatives into a position senior to depositors.

So let's just not bank on Congress protecting the interests of the American public (no pun intended). That doesn't mean we shouldn't fight like Hell to prevent the legislation when it is presented. But this assumes that the wording is not buried in some 2,000 page bill benefiting widows and orphans that is quietly passed by lawmakers in the middle of the night.

2. If you have deposits in one of the G-SIfIs, I recommend you move them. Try a good local credit union (the list of the Financial Stability Board's G-SIFIs can be found at the following link). http://regreformtracker. aba.com/2011/11/financial-stability-board-names-29. html (scroll to the bottom of the article and click the G-SIFI link).

Isn't it too cute that the planet's biggest banks get labeled as too big to fail? It doesn't matter what they do, the government will not let them fail and if the FDIC has its way, they will simply convert some of the their depositor's funds to stock to cover their losses. Shazam! Saved.

It is also noteworthy that many of these banks are packed to the pin stripes with derivatives.

3. Then again, it is quite possible that when the FDIC pushes its deposits to stock legislation, it could seek to expand the program's jurisdiction, enabling them to convert the deposits of any failed bank to stock. I'm just saying...

After all, the definition of a **systemically important financial institution** (SIFI) is a bank, insurance company, or other financial institution whose failure might trigger a financial crisis. That is a very broad definition.

It would take a "crisis" for such legislation to pass Congress. But these guys can create a financial crisis with the click of a mouse and then hold Congress hostage to panic and civil unrest until they coughed up legislation. It has only been a few years since Hammering

Hank Paulson slammed TARP through Congress during the 2008 financial crisis with threats of riots in the streets. TARP was a $300 billion gift to Wall Street investment banks, the fraternity from which he came.

A few people bitched. Nothing was done.

Regardless of any legislation now or in the future, you should be leery of any bank that is carrying derivatives on its balance sheet. Remember uncle Buffet's warning, they are "financial weapons of mass destruction."

Even if your bank isn't carrying derivatives, you need to be sure they are sound. The banks in Cyprus didn't fail because they had derivatives, they had other investments (Greek bonds) that went bad.

You can check the general health of your bank at www.bankrate.com or www.weissrating.com. The information at Bankrate.com is free, Weiss charges $20 for a report on a bank.

These sites give letter grades that are certainly better than having no data at all. However, they don't have data on interest rate swaps that the bank might be carrying, and they omit some other key analysis points. Still, they are better than nothing.

As noted above, credit unions can be a good alternative to a bank. They are often healthier than their bank cousins, though some carry derivatives as well. Both Bankrate and Weiss also have credit union ratings.

But mark well: these plans being put in place by the Bank for International Settlements and published by the FDIC are not idle "safeguards". They are being put in place for a reason. A banking crisis will come. Sooner or later, it will come. The entire global banking structure is sitting on the mother of all bubbles—a multi-trillion dollar derivatives casino, and when it explodes, all Hell will break loose.

Having your funds in a healthy financial institution will help protect them, particularly if/when the FDIC's plan to "convert deposits to stock" in failing banks goes into effect.

4. And finally, if you really want to do something about the criminally corrupt banking system and the banksters that control the world's financial structure, promote the concept, to legislators and others, of a monetary system based on products and real estate—a system whereby money represents actual production. That would eliminate inflation and deflation and send the global financial mafia into permanent retirement.

Meanwhile, keep your powder dry.

8
Bail-Ins Are Coming

There has been a great deal of speculation about a new global currency.

Various theories have been advanced, and "exposés" have revealed the coming conversion of dollars to a mysterious "Red" currency emerging from Asia like some enigmatic fiscal Phoenix.

None of these hidden agendas have ever materialized. But a new global currency is coming. It is on the march as we speak, but it is not quite what you think.

This New *Financial* World Order is driven by the fact that, after a 70-year-run, the dollar is exiting the world stage as the lead in that often misunderstood play, *The Global Reserve Currency*.

There are of course people and institutions behind this, not the least of which is that icon of global financial manipulation, the International Monetary Fund (IMF). So it is no surprise that the new global currency will be the SDR.

Say what?

SDR stands for Special Drawing Rights. It is the currency— created by the CIA in 1969—that is issued by the International Monetary Fund.

(For the CIA's creation of the SDR see: the "Secret" declassified memo of December, 9, 1965, see the our earlier coverage of this development in the previous *Crisis By Design: The Untold Story of the Global Financial*

Coup, quoted on page 125 and reprinted here:

SECRET

Increasing liquidity

Trade won't be able to grow, and the system will remain vulnerable to speculation unless there is regular growth in the international money supply.

Gold can't provide the needed increase: industrial and speculative demand is too high. U.S. payment deficits can't either: foreigners are unwilling to hold more dollars when we run large deficits and unable to increase net reserves by accumulating dollars when our deficits are small.

<u>*Our strategy is to supplement gold and dollars with a new international asset, Special Drawing Rights (SDR).*</u>*-[the <u>emphasis mine</u>]*

What does all of this mean?

The dollar being the world's reserve currency means that this is the currency that has been held—is held—by the central banks of the world to facilitate international trade.

The Japanese want to buy oil from Venezuela. They sell yen and use dollars to hand and pay for the oil. Venezuela keeps the dollars and uses them to buy wheat from Russia. If Venezuela had no dollars, they would have to convert some bolivars to dollars and then buy the wheat.

Dollars were (and, to a declining extent, still are) the currency of international trade. This circumstance originated in 1971 when Nixon, the U.S. hemorrhaging dollars like a pig in a slaughter house, closed the gold window—no more gold to foreign central banks in exchange for dollars.

This had been the arrangement, which emerged from the re-structuring of the global financial system in 1944 at Brentton Woods, New Hampshire: dollars, turned into the U.S by foreign central banks, could be exchanged for gold.

The dollar was *as good as gold.*

In 1971, Dick said, "No more."

But Nixon, who was a little to the right of Attila the Hun politically, did have some negotiating chops. He made a deal with the House of Saud: The U.S. would protect Saudi Arabia's oil fields, if they would require dollars for the sale of their oil.

Thus was born the term "Petro Dollar."

This spread to all trade in oil and then to virtually all international trade.

The Petro Dollar deal enabled the U.S. government to continue its jihad of deficit spending (spending more than it took in in tax revenues and borrowing the short-fall from Mister Fed) and then gushing greenbacks around the planet as if the U.S. Treasury had sprung some kind of colossal leak.

It also meant that the central banks of the world would need to continue to keep dollars on hand for the purchase of oil and other goodies.

Then, after a four-decade run, the Boys from Basel (the Bank for International Settlements) decided to lower the curtain.

(Note: If one were to sketch out an organizational chart of the power structure of international finance, it would include—roughly in order of ascending importance—the European Central Bank (ECB), the Bank of England, the World Bank, the U.S. Federal Reserve Bank (the Fed), the International Monetary Fund (IMF) and the Bank for International Settlements (BIS) with its newly anointed hit man, the Financial Stability Board). These are the *Dons* of the global financial mafia, and the BIS is the Godfather).

The Global Financial Crisis (GFC) of 2008–09 marked the beginning of the end of dollar dominance. Like Al Pacino in *The Godfather*, who quietly joined in the baptism of his godson in the cloistered environment of a lavish cathedral when he had unleashed the Corleone assassins on his enemies, the Global Financial Crisis was the signal from the Financial Stability Board, perched in their lavish offices at the BIS, to commence the attack on the dollar—to remove it as the global reserve currency. This was the unstated purpose of the GFC of 2008–09.

Since April of 2009, a growing amount of international trade has been conducted in currencies other than the dollar. Russia, China, India, Brazil and others are increasingly conducting this trade in their own currencies.

Such conduct would have been unheard of a decade ago.

As the dollar continues to get bypassed by the yuan, the ruble, the rupee and others in international trade, its status as the global reserve currency—the currency being held by central banks—is being slowly replaced by the SDR.

At a pace that does not alarm the markets, the SDR will fully replace the dollar as the global reserve currency. This is happening now and will continue at an increasingly rapid pace until the SDR is formally crowned.

In case you're wondering about the strength or backing of the SDR, it too is a fiat currency; the IMF just *prints them*. Like the dollar, the yuan, the euro or any other national currency, the SDR is nothing more than printing press money—or, these days, digital money. It is not backed by gold or any tangible asset.

The dollar will continue to be used and traded along with the euro and the yuan, but, like some A-list celebrity who overdosed on heroin one night at the Marmont Hotel , it will still work, but will no longer command the power, influence or respect it once had.

Meanwhile, the central banks of the world will be packed with SDRs minted by the IMF. Those same central banks will also be increasingly controlled by the despotic dictates of the Bank for International Settlements—the 900-pound gorilla orchestrating this coup from behind its towering curtain in Basel, Switzerland.

What does this mean at the street level?

For one thing, the U.S. government will have to stop its deficit spending. Congress will have to balance the budget and stop overspending and spewing dollars around the planet. Why? Because central banks won't have to hold them any longer—not like they have been.

That is what anyone with the intelligence God gave a grape would do.

Will Congress do it?

When Donald Trump gets a crew cut. They will continue to overspend. And they will continue to borrow the shortfall, forcing the interest rates on U.S. debt (Treasury Bills and Bonds) to escalate.

No more 2.9% auto loans and 4% home loans. Moreover, as the dollar declines, foreign products will get more expensive—think German cars, Japanese cars, Japanese electronics, clothing made in China, agriculture from South America.

But higher interest rates and more expensive foreign goods are not the primary point here.

There are other aspects of this coup that one needs to understand.

Of particular concern is the plan by the Bank of International Settlements to protect the major banks from collapse during the next Global Financial Crisis —and to do so at the expense of depositors.

The next crisis—coming soon to a planet near you —is imminent: as covered in the previous chapter, there are quadrillions in Mickey Mouse derivatives* on the balance sheets of the world's major banks; trillions in government debt here, there, everywhere; printing presses gone mad in the U.S., Europe, Japan and China.

(*For those that haven't read the previous chapter, the vast majority of derivatives are nothing more than bets banks place on the direction of interest rates. They have this fancy, often confusing, name but they amount to little more than a bank using depositor's funds at a global roulette wheel to place a bet on red or black [are rates going up or down?]. These bets are structured in the form of securities like stocks or bonds. They are called derivatives.)

The crisis is coming. And the global banks would likely implode when it hits...except that the Financial Stability Board, the BIS's Luca Brasi, has formulated regulations that enable banks to recapitalize themselves by garroting the depositors—taking the funds from depositor's bank accounts.

Once again, we covered this in the prior chapter, but it bears repeating: the "bail-in" strategy was piloted with the banking crisis in Cyprus last year. A bail-in is the activity of a bank taking its depositor's money when it goes insolvent and converting those funds to bank stock.

The depositor has no say in this.

This is opposed to a "bail out" where the government or some external entity covers the bank's losses. What brings this to our attention again is the communiqué issued November 16, 2014 from the G-20 meeting in Brisbane, Australia.

The G-20 is an international organization made up of the 20 leading industrial nations on the planet. If Earth has a Board of Directors, it is the G-20. But even the G-20 takes its orders from the BIS and its council in crime.

As one of the key items in their communiqué, the G-20 forwards the Financial Stability Board's agenda to establish bail-ins as an operating basis for what they call *Global Systematically Important Banks* when they experience severe losses.

International bankers love names like this. In their memorandums they refer these dominant global banks as G-SIBs.

Sounds like some kind of South American virus.

These are banks that regulators claim would cripple the financial system if they collapsed. So if they get in trouble (having made bad investment decisions), then new rules permit them to take their depositor's money to protect themselves.

Unbelievable.

The BIS knows these banks are buried in high-risk derivative ordure, and their first priority is to protect them. While business losses have traditionally always come from the firm's capital, its stock, this new structure puts the depositor's at risk.

You can find a list of G-SIBs here. For those of you in the U.S., you should note the inclusion (among others) of Bank of American, J.P. Morgan Chase, Wells Fargo, Citibank, and Goldman Sachs on the list.

http://en.wikipedia.org/wiki/
List_of_systemically_important_banks

You will no longer be assured of the return of your principal when you deposit money in the bank. Once placed in your account, the money is technically no longer "yours." You have lent it to the bank and you are a creditor. The bank owes you the money as if you had laid the carpet in the new branch lobby.

If the bank goes insolvent, they will be able to take some of your deposit and make themselves whole. Of course you get some of the bank's stock in lieu of your deposits. Who could ask for more? Stock in a failed bank instead of the money in the college fund you saved for your child's education.

These regulations also have a new basis in U.S. law. The ability of the FDIC to take your deposits in the case of a failed bank is set forth in the Obama administration's infamous Dodd-Frank Act, shepherded through Congress in 2010 by those icons of legislative befuddlement, Chris Dodd in the Senate and Barney Frank in the House.

Dodd and Frank both got out of Dodge after passage of the legislation—Frank to a teaching position at Harvard on gay and lesbian history and Dodd to the $3.3 million paycheck as the chief lobbyist for the movie industry.

The point being that the machinations of the druids at the BIS are now memorialized in U.S. law.

http://www.law.cornell.edu/wex/dodd-frank_titl

One simply needs to follow the dots.

1. This operation started in 2005. It was then that a revision of the U.S. bankruptcy laws placed holders of derivatives in a senior position to bank depositors.

In other words, if a bank goes insolvent, first dibs on the bank's assets belong to holders of derivatives. They are <u>ahead of the depositors.</u>

The following is from attorney and financial writer, Ellen Brown (www.ellenbrown.com), as quoted in the *Huffington Post*:

> *In the U.S., depositors have actually been put in a worse position than Cyprus deposit-holders, at least if they are at the big banks that play in the derivatives casino. The regulators have turned a blind eye as banks use their depositaries to fund derivatives exposures. And as bad as that is, the depositors, unlike their Cypriot confreres, aren't even senior creditors. Remember Lehman? When the investment bank failed, unsecured creditors (and remember, depositors are unsecured creditors) got eight cents on the dollar. One big reason was that derivatives counterparties require collateral for any exposures, meaning they are secured creditors. The 2005 bankruptcy reforms made derivatives counterparties senior to unsecured lenders. [Emphasis added.] http://www.huffingtonpost.com/ ellen-brown/banks-confiscation_b_2957937.html*

This put derivatives on top.

2. Step two occurred in 2010 when Congress passed the Dodd-Frank bill, which states explicitly that depositors are unsecured creditors.

http://www.law.cornell.edu/wex/dodd-frank_titl

3. In 2012, in a joint resolution, the FDIC and the Bank of England set forth the operating basis for financial regulators in their respective countries, that insolvent banks can take depositor's funds and convert them into bank stock.

https://www.fdic.gov/about/srac/2012/gsifi.pdf

(Remember, money deposited in the bank is no longer yours. It now belongs to the bank. You are a creditor).

4. The following year, 2013, as a pilot, the European Central Bank enforced this exact operating basis on two insolvent banks in Cypress. A senior regulator with the ECB issued a statement at the time that bail-ins would be the template used in future bank failures. (He later got his hand spanked, but he had revealed the planning.)

http://blogs.marketwatch.com/thetell/2013/03/25/
heres-the-gloss-on-those-dutch-ministers-cyprus-
comments/

5. On November, 2014, the G-20 confirmed the Financial Stability Board's regulations that depositor funds were subject to confiscation and conversion to bank equity (stock) by insolvent banks.

You think the BIS, the IMF and their surrogates in the U.S. Congress know something is coming? What really prompted these laws and regulations and why now?

U.S. banks currently hold $227 **trillion** dollars worth of derivatives. Over 90% of these are held by four major U.S. banks (G-SIBs): Bank of America, J.P. Morgan Chase, Goldman Sachs and Citibank. Wells Fargo is also a significant holder of derivatives.

Does it raise anyone's eyebrows that depositors are being set up to take the fall in the next financial crisis?

What to do?

1. If you maintain deposit accounts at any of the major global banks mentioned above, I suggest you move them. You are safer in a smaller, independent bank.

Even better, in most cases, a credit union can be a safer place to bank. This is generally true, though individual institutions, of course, vary. Membership in most credit unions is very flexible.

You can check out the strength of your bank at www. bankrate.com or at http://weissratings.com/products/banks.aspx

Bank Rate is free. Weiss Ratings charges $19.95 for its analysis.

If you need or want an in-depth professional analysis

of your current bank or a bank or credit union you are considering, or want help locating a bank or credit union to move to, contact the author to discuss services and fees: johntrumanwolfejr@gmail.com.

2. If you don't have any, get some precious metals. I know: the metals are in a bear market. I have recommended silver from the time that it was $5.00 per ounce all the way up to $40+ and also as it has trended down to the current $16 per ounce range. And gold from $300 an ounce up to $1,900 and as it has declined to the current price of about $1,200.

If you have some metals, I would not recommend acquisition of any more at this time. But do hang on to what you have.

However, if you don't, you should acquire some. Yes, even in a declining market. Put 10–20% of your assets into silver and gold.

Having some metals on hand remains sound insurance.

Despite the fact that central banks are avariciously acquiring gold "as we speak" and the printing of dollars is beyond imagining, the precious metals markets continue to decline and the dollar—unbelievably—has entered a new bull market.

How could this be?

It is no longer a secret that these markets are manipulated.

The major banks that the BIS is so intent on protecting from insolvency are manipulating both the currency and the precious metals markets and raking in billions in profits as they do so.

If you think the manipulation of the currency and precious metals markets are some kind of conspiratorial unreality, let me introduce you to the largest financial scandal in human history, which occurred just two years ago: the manipulation of Libor interest rates. ("Libor" stands for the London Interbank Offer Rate, which essentially is the base interest rate on which trillions of dollars of loans and investments are made in both the U.S. and abroad.)

You will recall the earlier description of derivatives as being mainly banks "betting" on the direction of interest rates. This global crap game deals in hundreds of **trillions** of dollars. What if those rates were being controlled? What if the gamblers—big banks—were placing the bets and then were able to manipulated the rates in their favor?

> *Because Libor is used in US derivatives markets, an attempt to manipulate Libor is an attempt to manipulate the US derivatives markets, and thus a violation of American law. Since mortgages, student loans, financial derivatives, and other financial products often rely on Libor as a reference rate, the manipulation of submissions used to calculate those rates can have significant negative effects on consumers and financial markets worldwide.*

> *In court documents filed in Singapore, Royal Bank of*

Scotland (RBS) trader Tan Chi Min told colleagues that his bank could move global interest rates and that the Libor fixing process in London had become a cartel. Tan, in his court affidavit, stated that the Royal Bank of Scotland knew of the Libor rates manipulation and that it supported such actions.

It has been reported since then that regulators in at least ten countries on three different continents are investigating the rigging of the Libor and other interest rates.[64][65] *Around 20 major banks have been named in investigations and court cases.*[66]

http://en.wikipedia.org/wiki/Libor_scandal

So, don't think for a second that the precious metals or currency markets are not manipulated. Indeed, in James Rickard's new book, *The Death of Money*, he documents the behind the scenes manipulation of the gold market in stunning detail by major gold trading banks (think J.P. Morgan), central banks, and facilitating it all, the Bank for International Settlements.

The same holds true for the stock market, which (based on buying and manipulation of stocks by central banks) is soaring to record highs almost daily.

Current estimates for the foreseeable future, despite all fundamentals to the contrary, are that the dollar will continue to rise, precious metals will continue to decline and the Dow Jones Industrial Average will continue its bull market ride into uncharted territory.

These conditions make no economic sense unless one understands that these markets are like puppets on strings. We can shake our heads in disagreement with the logic, but these are the current directions in which the strings are being pulled.

Still, make sure you have some precious metals.

3. Finally, acquire some real estate in the following categories: (A) multi-family real estate (duplex, triplex, etc.). It will provide income, tax benefits, and a home, if needed in the future. (B) If you have the opportunity, buy some agricultural land—land that is producing food. You can rent it out for the time being.

If you can do both, do so.

4. Stay liquid. Cash is king in times like these. Keep the money in safe financial institutions, and some in a good safe at home.

So, for now then: relocate savings out of any of the large banks mentioned above; acquire or retain precious metals; acquire income and agricultural producing real estate; stay liquid— cash.

There is of course, no guarantee with any of these recommendations. They are simply my best estimate of the situation at this time, based on my evaluation of the information in hand in a rapidly moving financial landscape.

That said, I don't expect Basel to pull the plug yet. My guess—and it is only a guess—is 18–24 months.

Maybe sooner. Maybe later. But be prepared.

John Truman Wolfe
December, 2014

ENDNOTES

Notes to Preface

[1] *"Our Nations' First TRUE Patriots."* From Bob Aldrich. KeelyNet. Keelynet.com. Web Jun 23, 2010.

[2] Rollins, Richard. *The Long Journey of Noah Webster*. Philadelphia: U. of Penn. Press, 1988.

Notes to Introduction

[1] Ney, Richard. *The Wall Street Gang: The book that tells you how to beat the Wall Street manipulators at their own game!* New York: Avon, 1974. Print.

[2] Warren, Ted. *How to Make the Stock Market Make Money for You*. Cutchogue, N.Y.: Buccaneer Books. 1994. Print.

[3] *See Confessions of an Economic Hit Man* by John Perkins. New York: Plume, 2004. Print.

[4] See "The Crash: Unraveling the Global Financial Crisis: Is the Worst Over?" PBS.org Frontline. Aug 5, 1997. Web. Oct. 10, 2009.

[5] See also Michel Chussodovsky. *"Financial Warfare: How The Biggest Banks Created A Global Crisis." Albion Monitor.* AlbionMonitor.com. Oct. 8, 1998. Web. Nov. 15, 2009.

[6] See "International Financial Crises and the IMF." Cato Handbook for 108th Congress. Cato.org. Jan. 16, 2003, Web. Nov. 10, 2009.

Notes to Chapter 1 "Behind the Wizard's Curtain"

[1] Paul Harvey, long-time radio broadcaster for ABC network debuted his radio show *The Rest of the Story*, and it continued until his death in February, 2009. *Wikipedia.com* Wikipemedia Foundation Inc. Web. Feb. 28, 2009.

[2] See Ralph G. Walton, Robert Hudak, and Ruth J. Green-Waite. "Adverse Reactions to Aspartame: Double-Blind Challenge in Patients from a Vulnerable Population." *Biol. Psychiatry* v.34 1993, 13–17. Print.

3   See Holmes, "Fannie Mae Eases Credit To Aid Mortgage Lending." *NY Times.com*. New York Times. Sept 30, 1999. Web. Nov. 10, 2008.

4   See *"Important Banking Legislation."* FDIC.gov. May 15, 2007. Web. Nov. 10, 2008.

5   See Kathleen Day, *"Greenspan Calls for Repeal Of Glass-Steagall Bank Law." pqasb.sparchiver.com*. The Washington Post. Nov. 19, 1987. Web. Nov. 10, 2008.

6   Engdahl. F. William. See "The Financial Tsunami and the Evolving Economic Crisis: Greenspan's Grand Design." *Global Research.ca*. Jan. 23, 2008 Web. Dec. 1, 2008.

7   See "Commodities Future Modernization Act of 2000." This act mandated that financial derivatives could be traded over the counter by financial institutions without regulations.

    See also James Moore, "A Nation of Village Idiots." James Moore. *Huffington Post.com*. Sept. 18, 2008. Web. Sept 18, 2008.

8   See Henry C.K. Liu. "Killer Touch for Market Capitalism." *AsiaTimesOnline.com*. Oct. 30, 2008. Web. Dec. 1, 2008.

9   See Liz Moyer and Hannah Clark. *"Paulson's Big Leap."* *Forbes.com*. Financial Services—Forbes. Jun. 1, 2006. Web. Dec. 1, 2008.

10 See graphic *"The Rescue Plan – The Largest Recipients." NYTimes.com*. Oct. 13, 2008. Web. Oct. 13, 2008.

11 See Gretchen Morgenson. *"Investors in Mortgage-Backed Securities Fail to React to Market Plunge." NYTimes.com*. Feb. 18, 2007. Web. Jan. 15, 2009.

12 See *"Dow Jones Industrial Average Chart."* Wikipedia. n.d. Web. Mar. 1, 2009.

13 See *"Financial Crisis of 2007 – 2010."* Wikipedia. n.d. Web. Mar. 1, 2009.

14 See Mary Kane. "Low Income Borrowers Made Scapegoat Amid Crisis." *WashingtonIndependent.com*. Sept. 30, 2008. Web. Dec. 5, 2008.

15 See Gordon Rayner. "Global Financial Crisis Does: Does the World Need a New Banking Policeman?" *Telegraph.co.uk* UK Telegraph. Oct. 8, 2008. Web. Oct. 8, 2008.

[16] Parker, Kenneth. "93% of Mortgages are Being Paid on Time." *www.t-g.com*. Shelbyville Times-Gazette. March 6, 2008. Web. Jan. 8, 2009.

[17] President Obama to the Joint Chiefs of Staff. www.whitehouse.gov. Feb. 24, 2009. Web. Mar. 1, 2009.

[18] See Tamara Keith. "Some Consumers See Credit Cards Cancelled." *NPR.org*. National Public Radio. Oct. 10, 2008. Web. Dec. 5, 2008.

[19] Quoted in Edmund Conway. *Telegraph.co.uk* Daily Telegraph, Dec. 15 2007. Web. Dec. 15, 2007.

[20] See Jacob Gerber. "Australia's January Manufacturing Index Shrinks for Eight Months. Bloomberg.com. Feb. 1, 2009. Web. Mar. 1, 2009.

See also "Industrial Production Still Falling." *ChinaTradeInformation.net*. China Trade News. June 12 2009. Web. Mar. 1, 2009.

See also "Japanese exports fall by the most in 7 years." *NY-Times.com*. Nov. 2, 2008. Web. Mar.1, 2009.

See also Lee Chyen Yee. "UPDATE 2-Taiwan export orders show Asia slump deepens." *Reuters.com*. Feb. 24 2009. Web. Mar. 1, 2009.

See also "South Korean Exports Fall Sharply." *Taipei-Times.com*. Dec. 2, 2008. Web. Mar. 1, 2008.

See also "Recession tipped as Singapore exports fall." *Channel-NewsAsia.com*. Sept. 17, 2008. Web. Mar. 1, 2008.

See also "Hong Kong's Exports Decline for a 12th Straight Month (Update2)." *Bloomberg.com*. Nov. 26, 2009. Web. Mar. 1, 2009.

See also "Export plunge leads record German GDP drop." *Irish-Times.com*. Feb. 25, 2009. Web. Mar. 1, 2009.

See also "List of recessions in the United Kingdom." *Wikipedia.com*. Web. Mar. 1, 2009.

[21] See Press Release. FederalReserve.gov. Oct, 6 2008. Web. Dec. 1, 2008.

[22] See Steve Watson. "Former Kissinger Policy Planner, CFR Member Calls For New Global Monetary Authority." *Infowars.net*. Sept. 26, 2008. Web. Nov. 15, 2009.

[23] See Peter Hartcher. "Obama's Economic Saviour Savaged as Keating Lets Rip." SMH.com. Sidney Morning Herald. Mar. 7, 2009. Web. Nov. 15, 2009.

[24] See "World Needs New Bretton Woods, says Brown." *AFP. com.* AFP. Oct, 13 2008. Web. Nov. 16, 2009.

[25] See M.J. Stephey. "Bretton Woods System." *Time.com.* Oct. 21, 2008. Web. Mar. 1, 2009.

[26] See Evelyn de Rothschild Global Financial Crisis 2008-2010. *www.global-financial-crisis.org.* Dec 10, 2008. CNBC video. Dec 12, 2008.

[27] See Dominique Strauss-Kahn. "The IMF and Its Future." *IMF.org.* International Monetary Fund. Speech at the Banco de España, Madrid, Spain. Dec. 30, 2005. Web. Dec. 12, 2008.

[28] See "After the Meltdown. A Private Roundtable on a New U.S. International Economic Policy." *AmericanProgress.org.* Dec. 22, 2008. Web. Dec. 12, 2008.

[29] Jaime Carauana is the General Manager for the Bank for International Settlements, a post he took April 1, 2009. Prior to that, he was the Director of the Monetary and Capital Markets Department of the IMF (July 2006 to April 2009.) Prior to that he was the governor of the Bank of Spain. The IMF is notorious for stirring the pot of financial unrest. The Bank of Spain had its finger in the pie of mortgage-backed securities traded as derivatives.

See Jaime Caruana's Biography. *Allvoices.com.* n.d. Web. Dec. 12, 2008.

See Derivatives Markets in Spain *ipyme.org* Gobierno de Espa a. n.d. Web. Dec. 12, 2008.

[30] Gordon Rayner. "Global Financial Crisis: Does the World Need a New Banking 'Policeman'?" *www. Telegraph.co.uk.* U.K. Telegraph. Oct 8, 2008. Web. Oct 8, 2008.

Notes to Chapter 2 "Hitler's Bank Goes Global"
[1] See Jane Macartney. "Compliments, Not Controversy, Mark Hillary Clinton's Beijing Visit." *Thetimes.co.uk.* The London Times. Feb. 23, 2009. Web. April 10, 2009.

2   "G20 Leaders Agree on Supervisory Body." *www.China daily.com*. China Daily. Apr. 3, 2009. Web. April 10, 2009.
    See also Natasha Brereton. "FSF Reestablished As FSB, Gets Stronger Mandate." *Fxstreet.com*. Fx. April 2, 2009. Web. April 10, 2009.

3   See Mario Draghi. "Re-establishment of the FSF as the Financial Stability Board." *Finanacialstabilityboard.org*. Financial Stability Board. Apr. 2, 2009. Web. May 14, 2009.

4   Mandate, *Financial Stability Board.org*. n.d.Web. March 31, 2009.

5   See Carroll Quigley. *Tragedy and Hope: A History of the World in Our Time*. San Pedro, C.A.: G. S. G. & Associates, Incorporated, 1975. Print.
    See also Higham, Charles. *Trading with the Enemy: the Nazi-American Money Plot 1933-1949*. Lincoln, N.E.: iUniverse, 2007 (1983). Print.
    See also Sutton, Anthony. *Wall Street and the Rise of Hitler*. Cutshogue, N.Y.: Buccaneer Books, 1974. Print.

6   Joan Veon, "Controlling the World's Monetary System: The Bank for International Settlements." *NewsWithViews.com*. News With Views. Aug. 26, 2003. Web. Mar. 14, 2009.

7   Dick Morris. "Ending American Sovereignty." *TheBulletin. us*. The Bulletin. Apr. 6, 2009 Web. May 5, 2009.

8   See speech by the Honorable Ron Paul, Congressional Record, 111th Congress, Page 502, *Thomas.loc.gov*. Library of Congress. Feb. 26, 2009. Web. April 10, 2009.

The Federal Reserve has the apparency of being a government entity. While created by the U.S. Congress in 1913, the Federal Reserve is an independent entity headed by a Board of Governors consisting of seven presidential appointees, confirmed by the Senate. And that is where the Congressional oversight ends. Although the Federal Reserve has many of the privileges of government agencies, it retains the benefits of being a private organization including being insulated from Freedom of Information Act requests. The Fed has broad powers including entering into agreements with foreign central banks and foreign governments, but the Government Accountability Office is prohibited from auditing or even seeing these agreements.

⁹ See "Interest Expense on the Debt Outstanding." *Treasury Direct. Gov*, Treasury Direct. n.d. Web Mar. 14, 2009.

¹⁰ "President Obama agreed at the G20 meeting in London to create an international board with authority to intervene in U.S. corporations by dictating executive compensation and approving or disapproving business management decisions. Under the new Financial Stability Board, the United States has only one vote. In other words, the group will be largely controlled by European central bankers." See Marilyn Barnewall. "What Happened to American Sovereignty at G-20?" *NewsWithViews.com*. News With Views. April 18, 2009. Web. Apr. 28, 2009.

¹¹ Ellen Hodgson Brown, J.D. "Big Brother in Basel: BIS Financial Stability Board Undermines National Sovereignty." *WebofDebt.com*. The Web of Debt. June 22, 2009. Web. April 24, 2009.

"Article II, Section 2 of the United States Constitution grants power to the President to make treaties only with the "advice and consent" of two-thirds of the Senate. The Constitution does not expressly provide for any alternative to the Article II treaty procedure. However, historically the President has also made international "agreements" through congressional-executive agreements that are ratified with only a majority from both houses of Congress, or sole-executive agreements made by the President alone. A congressional-executive agreement can cover only those matters which the Constitution explicitly places within the powers of Congress and the President; while a sole-executive agreement can cover only those matters within the President's authority or matters in which Congress has delegated authority to the President. A sole-executive agreement can be negotiated and entered into only through the President's authority (1) in foreign policy, (2) as commander-in-chief of the armed forces, (3) from a prior act of Congress, or (4) from a prior treaty. Agreements beyond these competencies must have the approval of Congress (for congressional-executive agreements) or the Senate (for treaties). *If an international commercial accord contains binding "treaty" commitments, then a two-thirds vote of the Senate may be required."*

12 See John C. Yoo. "Laws as Treaties?: The Constitutionality of Congressional-Executive Agreements." *eScholarhip.org.* University of California. Jun. 1, 2000. Web. April 10, 2009.

Notes to Chapter 3 "The Hidden Beginning"

1   See Thayer Watkins. "The Bubble Economy of Japan." Sjsu. edu. San José State University, Department of Economics. n.d. Web. May 1, 2009.

2   See Anthony Randazzo, Michael Flynn, and Adam B. Summers. "Avoiding an American 'Lost Decade': Lessons from Japan's Bubble and Recession." *Reason.org.* Reason Foundation. Feb. 2009. Web. May 10, 2009.

3   See Patrick S. J. Cormack and Bill Still *The Money Masters: How International Bankers Gained Control of America.* Ava Maria, FL: Royalty Production Company, 1998.

4   "Basel Committee: International Convergence of Capital Measurement and Capital Standards (Updated to April 1998)." *BIS.org.* Bank for International Settlements. July 1988. Web. May 1, 2010.

5   "Capital Requirements and Bank Behaviour: The Impact of the Basle Accord." *BIS.org.* Bank for International Settlements. April 1999. Web. May 1, 2010.

6   See Linda Allen. "The Basel Capital Accords and International Mortgage Markets: A Survey of the Literature." *NYU. edu.* Stern School of Business, New York University. Dec. 2003. Web. May 5, 2010.

7   See note 1 above.

8   "2nd LD: Nikkei Plunges Nearly 5%, Briefly Drops Below 8,000." *FreeLibrary.com.* Farlax. Jan 15, 1989. Web. May 5, 2010.

9   "Buffet warns on investment 'time bomb.'" BBC.co.uk. British Broadcasting Association. Mar. 4, 2003. WEB. May 28, 2009.

10 "Credit Default Swaps Explained." *EconomicsHelp.org.* Economics.Help. Nov. 11, 2008. Web. May 28, 2009.

11 See "Frank Partnoy: Derivative Dangers." NPR.org. National Public Radio. Mar. 25, 2009. Web. May 28, 2009. (Excerpt taken from Partnoy's book, *Fiasco: Blood in the Water on Wall Street.* New York: W.W. Norton, 2009.)

12 Kessler, Andy. "Have We Seen the Last of the Bear Raids?" WJS.com. Wall Street Journal. Mar. 26, 2009. Web. May 28, 2009.

Notes to Chapter 4 "The Goldman Connection"

1   Excerpts by Matt Taibbi. From *Rolling Stone*, July 9-23, 2009. © Rolling Stone LLC 2009. All Rights Reserved. Reprinted by Permission.

2   *Wall Street*, released Dec. 1987 by 20th Century Fox, directed by Oliver Stone. IMDB.com. The Internet Movie Database. n.d. Web. Sept. 1, 2009. Aug 1, 2009.

3   See Thomas M. Kostigen. "The 10 most unethical people in business." *Marketwatch.com.* Market Watch. Jan. 15, 2009. Web. Jan. 15, 2009.

4   See Julie Creswell and Ben White. "The Guys from 'Government Sachs'." *Nytimes.com.* The New York Times. Oct. 7, 2008. Web. July 15, 2009.

5   See Timothy Noah. "Robert Rubin's Free Ride." *Slate.com.* Slate. Jan. 9, 2009. Web. July 15, 2009.

6   "On The Edge with Max Keiser." *MaxKeiser.com.* Max Keiser internet financial program. July 3, 2009. Web. Aug. 6, 2009.

7   See "Barack Obama: Top Contributors" *OpenSecrets.org.* Center for Responsive Politics. July 13, 2009. Web. Aug. 1, 2009.

8   See David Lawder. "Paulson sees subprime woes contained." *Reuters.com.* Reuters. Aug 1, 2007. Web. Feb. 1, 2009.

9   See Randall Mikkelsen. "Banks sound but economy to take time: Paulson." *Reuters.com*. Reuters. Jul. 21, 2008. Web. July 15, 2009.

10 "FDIC-Insured Institutions Lost $3.7 Billion in the Second Quarter of 2009." FDIC.gov. Aug. 27, 2009. Web. Aug. 27. 2009.

11 See Alison Vekshin. "Bair Says Insurance Fund Could Be Insolvent This Year (Update1)." *Bloomberg.com*. Bloomberg. Mar. 4, 2009. Web. Mar. 4, 2009.

12 See Alison Vekshin and Dawn Kopecki. "Paulson Plans to Take Control of Fannie, Freddie (Update1)" *Bloomberg.com*. Bloomberg. Sep. 6, 2008. Web. Aug. 1, 2009.
    "Transcript for August 10, 2008." *Msnbc.msn.com*. Meet the Press. Aug. 10, 2008. Web. Aug. 1, 2009.

13 See Erik Holm. "AIG's bailout cost US$182.5-billion." *Bloomberg.com*. Bloomberg. Mar. 23, 2009. Web. Mar. 31, 2009.

14 See Jim Puzzanghera and Tom Hamburger. "Goldman Sachs defends $13-billion payment from AIG." *LATimes.com*. Los Angeles Times. Mar. 21, 2009. Web. Mar. 21. 2009.

15 An extrapolation. See Debra Bell. "10 Things You Didn't Know About AIG CEO Edward Liddy." *politics.usnews.com*. U.S. News and World Report. Mar. 18, 2009. Web. Aug. 1, 2009.

16 See "Inside the Meltdown." *PBS.Org*. Frontline. Feb. 17, 2009. Aug. 3, 2009.

17 Title 1–Troubled Assets Relief Program, Emergency Economic Stabilization Act of 2008. Pub. L. 110-343. Oct. 3, 2008. Stat. 122.3765.

18 See John Carney. "Merrill Lynch Paid More Than $3 Billion Bonuses After Suffering $27 Billion In Losses." *BusinessInsider.com*. Clusterstock. Jul. 30, 2009. Web. Aug. 8, 2009.

19 See Peter Barnes and Joanna Ossinger. "B of A to Get $20B More From TARP, Plus Backstop on $118B." *FoxBusiness.com*. Fox Business. Jan. 16, 2009. Web. Aug. 3, 2009.

[20] See Rick Rothacker. "Wachovia pays Goldman millions in fees." *CharlotteObserver.com*. The Charlotte Observer. Nov. 19, 2008. Web. Aug. 3, 2009.

[21] See note 1 above.

[22] See Andy Borowitz. "Goldman Sachs in Talks to Acquire Treasury Department." *HuffingtonPost.com*. The Huffington Post. Jul. 16, 2009. Web. Aug. 8, 2009.

[23] See note 1 above.

[24] "About Us." *WorldBank.org*. The World Bank. n.d. Web. Oct. 10, 2009. Aug 3, 2009.

[25] See James Bovard. "The World Bank Vs. the World Poor." Cato Policy Analysis No. 92. *Cato.org*. The Cato Institute. Sep. 28, 1987.

[26] See Anderson, Sarah. "The World Bank and IMF's Cosmetic Makeover." *Dollarsandsense.org*. Dollars & Sense Magazine. Jan./Feb. 2001. Web. March 15, 2009.

[27] See William McQuillen. "Wolfowitz's New Job Turning Him Into Iraq War's Invisible Man." *Bloomberg.com*. Bloomberg. Dec 7, 2005. Web. Aug. 3, 2009.

   Robert McNamara was one of, if not the, masterminds behind the Vietnam War. See Thomas Lippman. "'Terribly Wrong' Handling of Vietnam Overshadowed Record of Achievement." *Washington-Post.com*. The Washington Post. Jul. 7, 2009. Web. Aug. 3, 2009.

Notes to Chapter 5 "Preparing for a Money Meltdown"

[1] See "The Daily History of Debt Results." TreasuryDirect. gov. *Treasury Direct*. Oct. 2009. Web. Oct. 2, 2009.

[2] See statement from speech *"Storms on the Horizon."* Remarks by Richard W. Fisher, CEO Federal Reserve Bank of Dallas, before the Commonwealth Club of California, San Francisco, California. www.DallasFed.org. May 28, 2008. Web. Oct 2, 2009.

[3] Do the math. One dollar = 6", 2 = 1ft. I trillion dollars = 500 billion feet. 5,280 ft in one mile = 97,696,969 miles. Speed of sound = 768 mph. One year = 6,727,680 miles. 14.52 years.

See Cybe. "What is a Trillion Dollars" *100777.com: A Site for Truthseekers.* 100777.com. Sept. 17, 2003. Web. Oct 2, 2009.

4   See Josiah Ryan. "Uncle Sam Will Pay $450 Billion This Year Just to Cover Interest on National Debt." *CNSNews. com.* Cybercast News Service. Dec. 16, 2008. Web. Oct 3, 2009.

5   See Rick Klein. "Dem Senator: Second Stimulus 'Probably Needed." *Abcnews.com* ABC News. July 6, 2009. Web. Oct 3, 2009. Web. Oct 3, 2009.

6   See Neil Roland. "Barney Frank: TARP's Comp Curbs Could be Extended to All Businesses." *Financial Week.com.* Financial Week. Feb. 3, 2009. Web. Oct. 2, 2009.

7   See Elizabeth Howard. "Capitol Offenses." *Middle America News.* Dec. 2008. Web. Jan. 15, 2009.

8   See "Targeting Your 401(k)." *Wall Street Journal.com/Opinion Journal.* Nov. 1 4, 2008. Web. Jan. 15, 2009.

9   See Matt Moffett. "Argentina Makes Grab for Pensions Amid Crisis." *Wall Street Journal.com.* Oct. 22, 2008. Web. Oct. 5, 2009.

10 See note 9 above.

11 See Duarte, Joe. "Argentina's Pension Grab Sets Dangerous Precedent." *FinancialSense.com* Financial Sense Editorials. Oct 23, 2008. Web. Oct. 5, 2009

12 Evans-Pritchard, Ambrose. Argentina seizes pension funds to pay debts. Who's next? *Telegraph.co.uk.* U.K. Telegraph. Oct. 21, 2008. Web. Oct. 5. 2009.

13 "Executive Order 6102." U.S. President, Franklin D. Roosevelt. *Wikipedia.com.* n.d. Web. Oct. 5, 2009.

14 "Currency Control." *Wikipedia.com.* n.d. Web. Oct. 5, 2009.

15 Casey, Doug . "The Casey International Speculator." *www. CaseyResearch.com.* The Casey Report. January, 2009. Web. January, 2009.

Notes to Chapter 6 "What You Can Do About It."

[1] Crutsinger, Martin "G-20 Leaders Push Global Economic Reforms Friday." *WDTN.com* Wdtn2. Sept. 25, 2009. Web. Oct. 28, 2009.

[2] "Special Drawing Rights (SDRs)." *Imf.org.* International Monetary Fund. Jan 31, 2010. Web. Oct. 28, 2009.

[3] "The CIA Chimes In On Gold Control; Highlights Historical Gold-To-Foreign Holdings Short funding." Bear Market Investments.com. September 26, 2009. Web.

[4] "Gold and the Gold Standard." *fsmitha.com.* Macro History and World Report. n.d. Web. Nov. 1, 2009.

[5] Barisheff, Nick. "August 15, 1971: Inflation Unleashed." *Kitco.com* Kitco. May 5, 2006. Web. Nov. 1, 2009.

[6] Actual recording of President Johnson talking to Robert McNamara. *americanradioworks.publicradio.org.* April 30, 1964. Web. Nov. 5, 2009.

[7] "Gulf of Tonkin Incident." *Wikipedia.com.* n.d. Web. Nov. 5, 2009.

[8] "Robert McNamara Deceived LBJ on Gulf of Tonkin." *Raw-Story.com* July 8, 2009. Web. Nov. 5, 2009.

[9] "FRED graphs." *http://research.stlouisfed.org.* Federal Reserve. 1918 to 2010. Web. Nov. 6, 2009.

[10] Nelson, Edward. "Milton Friedman and U.S. Monetary History: 1961-2006." *Research.StLouisFed.org.* Federal Reserve Bank of St. Louis *Review.* May/June 2007. Web. Oct. 15, 2009.

[11] Batini, Nicoletta and Nelson, Edward. "The Lag from Monetary Policy Actions to Inflations: Friedman Revisited." *BankofEngland.co.uk.* 2001. Web. Oct. 15, 2009.

[12] "Deposits." FDIC.gov. n.d. Web. Nov. 6, 2009.

[13] Hundley, Tom. "Oil Rich Norway Guards Its Wealth." *SeattleTimes.nwsource.com.* Seattle Times. Nov. 20, 2007 Web. Nov. 6, 2009.

[14] Hundley, Tom. "Oil Rich Norway Guards Its Wealth." *SeattleTimes.nwsource.com.* Seattle Times. Nov. 20, 2007 Web. Nov. 6, 2009.

ABOUT THE AUTHOR

John Truman Wolfe is the author of award-winning fiction and nonfiction books and articles including, "The Financial Crisis: A Look Behind the Wizard's Curtain," *America the Litigious*, *Mind Games*, *The Gift*, and his latest stunning release—*Crisis By Design: The Untold Story of the Global Financial Coup and What You Can Do About It*.

He has been a senior credit officer for two California banks: one in the San Francisco Bay Area, the other in Beverly Hills, and is the co-founder of a prestigious Los Angeles-based business-management company, where, as a registered investment advisor, he oversaw the financial and investment matters of some of the biggest names in Hollywood.

Shortly after the fall of Communism, John made several trips to Moscow giving seminars to leading bankers and senior members of the Russian government. In recognition of his work, government officials commissioned a sculpture of his bust by the noted Russia sculptor, Sergi Bychkov, which was placed in the Hall of Heroes of the Ministry of Internal affairs. Just prior to publication, Chinese government officials flew him to Beijing to consult with them on the causes and solutions to the global financial crisis. He spent several days in Beijing discussing the information revealed in *Crisis by Design* with these parties as well as doing media interviews for Chinese Television.

He has a Master's Degree with Honors from San Jose State University and is the former Chairman of the Department of History at John F. Kennedy University.

For more information, please visit www. BehindtheWizardsCurtain.com or www.Crisisby Design.net.

ACKNOWLEDGMENTS

To my wife, Barbara, who has been the sounding board for all my writing. She has a wonderful sense of style and has no problem suggesting revisions where she thinks they may be helpful or lavishing praise on the metaphorical morsels that delight her.

Thank you goes to the people who helped me fill in the research for this book. Everything I have said in this book is all over the Web, but it helps to have people who know how to find it. Karen Walby, Kurt Wilson, the Armchair Survivalist, Mitch Hermann, Alex Serrano, and Jim Criscoe, all stepped up and hit it out of the park. Thank you, too, Wendy Bellinger, for doing a last minute proof as we pushed the book out the door.

Thanks to the creative Kendra for the telling graphic in the Goldman chapter.

A special thanks to Boris Levitsky whose original vision it was to create a book out of the articles. Without his foresight, this never would have happened.

To Patricia, George, and Nick (the book's designer), whose dedication to publishing this book has exhausted all of the midnight oil in both Colorado and Southern California.

And finally, I'd like to thank Al Gore for inventing the Internet, because it is the ultimate research tool for the writer of nonfiction. I would also like to thank him for inventing global warming and carbon credits as a solution to the problem—not because it will make him billions but because this may turn out to be the biggest con job of all time, and will be the subject of my next article.

CPSIA information can be obtained
at www.ICGtesting.com
Printed in the USA
LVOW04s2137200416

484600LV00011B/63/P

9 780996 968645